PRAISE FOR PHIL COUSINEAU AND
THE ART OF PILGRIMAGE

"*The Art of Pilgrimage*—that's a classic." —Deepak Chopra, author of *Spiritual Solutions*

"Stories, anecdotes, quotes, vignettes, and practical suggestions from travelers and pilgrims throughout history create a guide to building a personal journey by learning to slow down and linger, savor, and absorb each stage." —*Library Journal*

"This book made me wish I could retrace my footsteps with Joe [Campbell] when we traveled the world together." —Jean Erdman Campbell, dancer and choreographer

"The discussions on Cousineau's *Global Spirit* series are sorely needed in this dispirited and disenchanted world." —Bill Moyers

"The quintessential traveling companion." —*Spirituality and Practice*

"Of all the books I've ever read about pilgrimage, this is the most poetic, personal, and timely." —John O'Donohue, author of *Anam Cara*

"I have made pilgrimages all my life. One, along the sea-roads of Charles Darwin, consumed more than 20 years. Then I found Phil Cousineau and now he is my guide on every wandering." —Georgia I. Hesse, founding travel editor, *San Francisco Examiner*

"A treasure. It triggers the imagination and memory of all inner and outer journeys one has or has not taken." —Angeles Arrien, PhD, cultural anthropologist and author of *The Four-Fold Way* and *Signs of Life*

"A must read before a trip." —*Escape*

"If Phil Cousineau's fine book were to have the influence it deserves, tourism might cease to be an environmental blight and become an educational blessing." —*San Francisco Chronicle*

"If Joseph Campbell, the Dalai Lama, and Bill Moyers were to have collaborated on a book about journeys I suspect it would look very much like *The Art of Pilgrimage*." —*Austin American Statesman*

"Seeking answers to one's own existence? Cousineau guarantees that the pilgrimage approach is the right path for obtaining those answers." —Brad Hooper, *Booklist*

"Whatever your longing, path, or destination, Phil Cousineau gives you the most valuable gear you could pack in your satchel." —Anthony Lawlor, author of *A Home for the Soul* and *The Temple in the House*

"Phil Cousineau's lifetime of pilgrimage has taken him from the depths of lost jungles to the heights of the human soul, always with passion, curiosity, warmth, wisdom, and humor." —Mort Rosenblum, author of *The Secret Life of the Seine* and *Olives: Life and Lore of a Noble Fruit*

"There is no better guide to the personal pilgrim's path than Phil Cousineau." —Alexander Eliot, author of *The Timeless Myths*

"Phil Cousineau—poet, scholar, contemporary man, free spirit—is at his best in *The Art of Pilgrimage*." —Robert A. Johnson, author of *Balancing Heaven and Earth*

"Phil Cousineau speaks to the heart of every genuine seeker with inspiring insight." —Rev. Stephen Gross, OFM Conv., rector of the Shrine of St. Francis of Assisi, San Francisco, CA

"What an incandescent journey! Every page yields brilliant treasures." —John Nance, author of *The Gentle Tasaday*

THE ART OF PILGRIMAGE

THE SEEKER'S GUIDE TO MAKING TRAVEL SACRED

PHIL COUSINEAU

FOREWORD BY HUSTON SMITH

Conari Press

First published in 1998 by
Conari Press, an imprint of Red Wheel/Weiser, LLC
With editorial offices at:
665 Third Street, Suite 400
San Francisco, CA 94107
www.redwheelweiser.com

Cover design: Jim Warner
Book design: Suzanne Albertson

ISBN: 978-1-57324-593-7

Library of Congress Cataloging-in-Publication Data available upon request.

Printed in the United States of America
MAL
10 9 8 7 6 5 4

To Richard Beban,
fellow pilgrim

Art is here taken to mean knowledge realized in action.
—René Daumal

PILGRIM, **n.** A traveler that is taken seriously.
—Ambrose Bierce

One cannot divine nor forecast the conditions
that will make happiness;
one only stumbles upon them by chance,
in a lucky hour, at the world's end somewhere,
and holds fast to the days. . . .
—Willa Cather

CONTENTS

FOREWORD

THE OBJECT OF PILGRIMAGE IS NOT REST AND RECREATION—to get away from it all. To set out on a pilgrimage is to throw down a challenge to everyday life. Nothing matters now but this adventure. Travelers jostle each other to board the train where they crowd together for a journey that may last several days. After that there is a stony road to climb on foot—a rough, wild path in a landscape where everything is new. The naked glitter of the sacred mountain stirs the imagination; the adventure of self-conquest has begun. Specifics may differ, but the substance is always the same.

Travel brings a special kind of wisdom if one is open to it. At home or abroad, things of the world pull us toward them with such gravitational force that, if we are not alert our entire lives, we can be sucked into their outwardness. Attentive travel helps us to see this, because the continually changing outward scene helps us to see through the world's pretensions. With its phantasmagoric, kaleidoscopic character laid bare, we see it for what it truly is—perpetually perishing *maya*— and the world loses its wager. We can understand how perpetual wandering can be a spiritual vocations, as with dedicated pilgrims and *sannyasins*.

❀ ❀ ❀

As Phil Cousineau has recently published a book on synchronicity, he can hardly object if I weave my Foreword around an instance of it.

When his invitation to contribute a foreword reached me and I was wondering what I might say, the answer jumped out at me from the closing pages of the book I was reading, Ursula Hegi's *Stones from the River*. Set in Nazi Germany during World War II, it is about a misfit, a dwarf named Trudi whose entire life is a longing to belong. As a child she would hang from doorframes for hours, hoping that the weight of her body would stretch its length. When it became apparent that her head was growing disproportionately large for her body, she wrapped it so tightly in bandages that it ached mercilessly the entire night. To no avail, of course.

When a circus with a dwarf named Pia came to town, Trudi was ecstatic. She was not alone! There was someone else in the world who was like her. During the circus days she sought out Pia at every opportunity, and Pia responded. She told her stories of a land where everyone was little. When the circus left, Trudi begged Pia to take her along, but Pia told her she belonged where she was.

The years go by. Trudi risked her life to help fugitives from the Nazis, and (as someone whose difference made her exceptionally understanding) she became the ears of the town as people poured out their troubles to her.

One evening toward the close of her life, instead of cooking her evening meal, Trudi climbed onto her bicycle and rode out to a dilapidated mill that had not been rebuilt. There, her preceding night's dream of her loving and ever-supportive father, recently dead, came back to her:

> *It hit her so strongly, that she crouched right where she was and brought her arms around her middle. The scent of chamomile enveloped her, and as she looked down, the tiny flowers were right in front of her, their yellow centers ringed by white petals. The closer she looked, the more she saw, and the more she forgot herself and her pain and became part of something she couldn't define, as if, by getting closer to a smaller world, she had found a larger world. How many times had she longed for a world where she knew she belonged? How often had she imagined living on the island of the little people? Yet, all she had needed was here,*

already here. Pia had been right—this was where she belonged.
Despite the horror of war. Because of its horror. Working with
the underground and the fugitives had taught her what it was
like to belong. That you could initiate it, build it, be it.

With that insight Trudi reached her destination, her life's goal.
But though pilgrimage is always an inward journey—in Trudi's case
it was entirely inward, for travel was closed to her—it helps to objec-
tify it by holding it at arm's length, so to speak. So target a distant
place—your Mecca, your Jerusalem, your Mount Meru—and set out.
You needn't don a hairshirt, for obstacles enough will erupt. But by
attending to them now—openness, attentiveness, and responsiveness
are the essence of pilgrimage—you will be able to surmount them by
yielding to them in the way that life always requires that we yield to
it. And draw the resilience you will need from those who have preceded you, for pilgrims are a hardy breed. They trudge rough roads,
put in long days, and live on breadcrusts. But hunger turns those
crusts into gourmet fare, and pilgrims sleep well from their fatigue,
even when their beds are hard ground and stones are their pillows.
On clear nights the stars that steer them cover them with their
canopy and token the eternal.

What can we learn from them, these pilgrims who have preceded
us? Much, but I will content myself with a passing point or two.

They tell us to be prepared to discover that from the spiritual point
of view a journey is always something of a two-edged sword because of
the dispersion which can result from contact with so much that is new.
We cannot simply shut ourselves off from this newness or we might
just as well stay at home—if we are going to travel we naturally wish
to learn something. But if the newness threatens to overwhelm us, it

can occasion periodic hardenings of the ego, as if in reaction to the fear of losing ourselves through dispersal we find it necessary to shore up our identities. The smallness of these identities is certain to bring suffering, however, beginning with feelings of impatience and annoyance. The art is to learn to master today's unavoidable situation with as much equanimity as we can muster, in preparation for facing its sequel tomorrow.

In the course of this training we come to see quite plainly how essential it is to have a purchase on our surroundings by being centered in ourselves, not somewhere in the outer world. The person who is always expecting consolation from without is like a swaying reed or a boat on a stormy sea. It seems as if in some uncanny way the surrounding world, the cosmic *maya*, senses this and loves to play with us—without malice to be sure, yet with a touch of mockery. To catch onto this trickery is a mark of sanctity.

Enough. Keeping in mind these token gleanings from those who have gone before, welcome to *The Art of Pilgrimage*. With his characteristic exuberance, expansiveness, and flair, Phil Cousineau captures all of the above and more in the pages that follow.

Dawn is breaking. It's time to head out.

Huston Smith
Professor of Religious Studies
University of California at
        Berkeley
June 1998

Preface to the New Edition

A S AN AVID TRAVELER AND ENTHUSIASTIC TRAVEL LEADER, I was struck by a mid-nineties United Nations report that projected by the year 2000 travel would become the number one business in the world. There was a veritable flurry of responses to the report speculating on what contributed to such a precipitous rise in travel in our time: lower transportation costs, faster airplanes, better guidebooks, increased safety in hotels and on the road. But the suggestion that caught my eye was a study that said it was the rise in pilgrimage—transformative travel to sacred places—that was the most dramatic reason of all. More people were taking the old "glory roads" to Rome, Jerusalem, Canterbury, Mecca and Medina, Borobodur, Angkor Wat, and Mount Kailas than at any other time since the Middle Ages. Once alerted to the word and to the phenomenon, I fell upon several more secular references in newspapers, magazines, and daily conversation: A trip to the Baseball Hall of Fame in Cooperstown, New York was a "pilgrimage"; a visit to James Joyce's Dublin was a "walk around"; a romp with the bulls in Pamplona, Spain was a long-standing tradition. I heard a war veteran describe his cross-country trip to Washington, D.C. to rub his hands over the names of his fallen friends at the Vietnam Veterans Memorial as his personal pilgrimage. When I read about a Japanese tour group visiting the Hewlett-Packard garage in Silicon Valley, the symbolic origins of the computer industry, as a pilgrimage, I felt I had to write about the unfolding phenomenon.

The Art of Pilgrimage was a personal response to the sea change in how modern people are traveling. The deeper I delved into the story, the more I realized how often I had been unknowingly using many of the same techniques that traditional pilgrims use, such as contemplating intention and practicing deep attention, taking gifts and leaving stories behind. In over twenty years of leading tour groups around the world and taking copious notes, I had made repeated reference to the alarming number of travelers I had encountered on the back roads of the world who were despondent about their experience, even angry about their perceived meaninglessness of their journey.

My book evolved into a model for people seeking another way to travel, a simple model to help them find more purpose and more meaning, even more connection to the countless generations of those who have traveled before us.

The response to *The Art of Pilgrimage* has been deeply gratifying. It has generated a boxcar load of handwritten letters, a raft of postcards, and clouds of emails, from Iceland to Antarctica. I have been blessed to hear from travelers who have carried dog-eared copies of the book with them on their journeys, such as the man who wrote to me from the trail to Machu Picchu in search of his Inca ancestral roots, or the two Australian nuns who wrote me while aboard a tramp steamer because they'd been inspired by the stories in the book to visit Angkor Wat and see it with their own eyes.

I heard from a family whose father was dying of cancer and had never spoken about his role as a bomber pilot in the Dresden firebombing during World War II. Together, they believed he needed some catharsis about his role, but they had no word for what needed to be done—until they read Pilgrimage, which inspired them to visit Dresden. This pilgrimage allowed their father closure on that episode from his past.

One day I received a packet of letters from school kids on Iona who were using the book to help guide them in their pilgrimage. They asked me if I would take them somewhere in the world. I said I would. When I asked them to choose where we'd be traveling to in a follow-up letter, they said, "No, where would you like to take us?" I suggested Greece, and a year later I was co-leading twenty-two sixteen-year-olds from All

Saints Church, in Atlanta, through the footsteps of Homer, Alexander, Sappho, and Saints John and Paul.

Over the years, many people have also written to me expressing astonishment that pilgrimage wasn't an outmoded and pious form of travel, but a timeless model of respectful and reverential journeying. I treasure my letters from the Winnebago Road Man, Reuben Snake, essayist Pico Iyer, language maven Alberto Manguel, Ed Tick and Kate Dahlstedt, who take war veterans on pilgrimage back to the sites of their trauma. Hall of Fame broadcaster Ernie Harwell called to tell me he wished he'd had the book when he and wife Lulu traveled to Jerusalem.

In 2002, I co-led a tour around the ancient sites in County Clare and Connemara in Ireland with the redoubtable ex-Catholic priest, poet, and scholar John O'Donohue. One day, John said to me, "You know, the revival of pilgrimage is the revival of modern Ireland." Mike Pinder, founding member of the Moody Blues, told me that Joseph Campbell's Hero's Journey and the pilgrimage model helped him realize there was life after rock and roll. Once, Joey Reynolds, long-time running midnight radio host in New York, asked me to stay on the line after our show ended because the legendary guitar player Les Paul was going to be joining him. When Mr. Paul wondered whether he had ever been on a bona fide pilgrimage I asked if he'd ever gone out of his way to go somewhere to honor the musical greats he admired. Immediately and excitedly, he said, "Oh, I do that every year when I go back to Kansas City and walk in their footsteps. Then I try to play something in their honor. Is that what you mean by pilgrimage?" Yes, I said, that's exactly it. Pilgrimage means following in the footsteps of somebody or something we honor to pay homage. It revitalizes our lives, reinvigorates our very souls.

More recently, a physician involved in taking eye doctors to India to perform free operations told me that he has shared the pilgrimage idea with fellow doctors, which helped them view their work through a new lens.

Over the last fourteen years, I've heard from soldiers who told me they were inspired to look at their time in war zones as a pilgrimage through the dark night of the soul. Those incarcerated in prisons have written me to share that they use hand-sized labyrinths to trace the pilgrimage of their day along the grooves of its passages. A guard who played with the Green Bay Packers thanked me for a model he could use as a psychotherapist for retired athletes. A ten-year-old cancer patient told me that when she got well, she was going to walk the Camino across Spain, in thanks for surviving. A Cincinnati woman with an autistic daughter informed me that the pilgrimage model helped her endure and then enjoy her difficult life with her little girl.

For those of you about to embark on your own pilgrimage, your own sacred journey, I pass on to you what an old Irish poet once told me on the cliffs of the Aran Islands: "We should all be grateful for the beauty of this world, but more, we should take the trouble to get off the bus of life and put the soles of our feet to the soul of the world and see those sacred sites with our own eyes."

Travel safely, travel soulfully, travel gratefully, and as the old pilgrim's advice goes, "Stranger, pass by that which you do not love."

Phil Cousineau
San Francisco, 2012

INTRODUCTION

IHAVE BEEN ON THE ROAD ALL MY LIFE. When I was only two weeks old, my parents bundled me into their 1949 Hudson and drove thirty straight hours from the army hospital where I was born, at Fort Jackson in Columbia, South Carolina, to Detroit, where I grew up. That early journey set the peripatetic pace for my wanderings.

As a family, we took trips whenever possible. My father was convinced that travel was good for the mind, while my mother believed it good for the soul. Our adventures were wide-ranging, from nostalgic visits to the ancestral family farm in northern Ontario to weekend drives to faraway museums, homes of inventors, and tombs of famous authors. They were great getaways, but the trip that stands out for me was one my father planned especially for my benefit, to the Baseball Hall of Fame in Cooperstown, New York. That visit to my pantheon of heroes was as powerful as later journeys to Delphi, Ephesus, or Jerusalem. It was a waking dream to walk on the hallowed ground where, according to legend, my favorite game was first played. I was awestruck at the chance to see the great relics of baseball: Babe Ruth's bat, Ty Cobb's spikes, and Shoeless Joe Jackson's glove.

After graduating from university in 1974, I undertook the rite of passage for thousands of my generation by recreating the old Grand Tour of Europe. Tramping over the cobblestones and riding the rails of the Old World for six glorious months lit a fire in my soul. I became so enthralled with the marvels of ancient history that I sent a telegram to my family explaining that I wouldn't be coming home for a long while. I told them I had never felt so alive, and wanted to try to live somewhere for a stretch before going back and embarking on a career. In truth, I dreaded the idea of returning home.

I found a small room in a boardinghouse in Kilburn, in the north of London, and worked at an array of odd jobs for six months until I'd

A young Bedouin camel driver offers a jaunty ride to a wayward traveler. Behind him looms the Great Pyramid of Cheops, near Giza, Egypt.

saved enough to start all over. To paraphrase Henry David Thoreau, I longed to travel deliberately, to encounter the "essential things" of history, venture somewhere strange and unknown, ancient and elemental.

One day, I passed a travel poster for Egypt in the window of an airline office near Marble Arch, and my pulse raced with the thrill of recognition. I had fantasized about exploring the world of the pharoahs since childhood. I felt beckoned.

Overwhelmed by the immensity of the ancient history looming before me, I prepared assiduously, seeking out the old Egyptology rooms at the British Museum and reading arcane books on archaeology and mythology discovered in musty old bookstores along Charing Cross Road.

But as the day of my departure for Cairo loomed closer, I was overwhelmed with anxiety. The night before I was to leave, Ahmet, a young

Egyptian who was also living in the boardinghouse, approached to wish me well on my journey. He asked me why I had chosen to travel to his homeland, what purpose I had. Taken aback, I paused for a moment, then told him I'd seen an exhibition, "The Art of Egypt's Sun Kings," at the Detroit Institute of Arts when I was in college and it had haunted me ever since. Now I wanted to see with my own eyes "where it all began," meaning civilization itself. Suddenly, I recalled something else, a photograph from the exhibition that burrowed into my memory, a black-and-white image of the archaeologist Howard Carter taken at the moment he opened the tomb of Tutankhamen in 1923. In that picture, which I still have hanging on my writing room wall, Carter's expression isn't one of greed at the sight of gold artifacts, but radiance from the revelation of a sacred mystery. Instantaneously, I knew what I was seeking: not just a surfeit of impressions, the casualty of modern travel, but a glimpse of an ancient mystery.

Ahmet nodded gracefully, then extracted a small piece of cardboard from his pack of Gauloise cigarettes. On it he wrote some words in Arabic script which looked like birds in flight:

Be Safe and Well   سَالَم

Peace, Love, Courage   شَجَاعة غَب فـكَاى

"This is the traditional farewell among my people for those leaving on a pilgrimage," he explained. At first, I was startled by his description of my upcoming trip. The word *pilgrimage* sounded arcane, even pious, suggesting a long-forgotten lesson from catechism class. Strange to say, as he spoke about his favorite archaeological sites along the Nile, the reverence with which he used the term enabled it to hover in my imagination. I remember him saying that making a pilgrimage was a way to prove your faith and find answers to your deepest questions. That stymied me; it forced me to ask myself what *I* believed in so strongly. But as Ahmet wrote down some names of friends and remote archaeological sites that would give me a sense of "the soul of the land," I realized that the word *pilgrim* captured what I had been secretly hoping to accomplish with my travels.

As we stood there in the dark hallway, I could smell tea brewing downstairs and hear the sound of trains rumbling from the nearby Tube station. Slowly, the thread of connection appeared between my boyhood journeys with my family and my recent wanderings to sacred sites such as Chartres Cathedral, the megalithic stones of Cornwall, the home where James Joyce was born, the healing waters of Lourdes, and the trenches of Flanders where millions died in the slaughter of World War I. My parents had instilled in me an appreciation for the soulful things in life—the world's sublime mysteries—and the fascination still burned in me.

Over the next few weeks, as I climbed the Cheops pyramid at midnight, explored the thrilling chaos of monumental sculpture in the Cairo museums, and sailed down the Nile in an azure blue felucca, Ahmet's words came back to me again and again. One afternoon, after exploring the tombs in the Valley of the Kings across the river from the vast ruins of Karnak, I wandered for hours in the desert sands nearby, a white bandanna wrapped around my head to protect me from the fiery sun. Alone, I stumbled through the tumbledown ruins of unnamed temples until I came across a group of Bedouins sitting in the shade of towering date trees. With supreme grace, they invited me to sit with them. They poured the finest mint tea I ever hope to drink. Patiently, they pointed out hieroglyphics on the fallen columns and explained the symbols for heart, eye, and the soul. The oldest among them slipped a wrinkled photograph out of his *djellaba* for me to see. He pointed at a young man laboring on an archaeological dig, then back at himself and at the rubble all around us. He was letting me know that many years before he had participated in the excavations of the temple grounds. A smile spread across his swarthy face as he made digging ges-

For more than forty centuries, the Sphinx at Giza has cast its enigmatic gaze across the desert, while the Pyramids of Chephren (left) and Cheops (right) have come to symbolize the mysterious human urge for monument-building.

tures with his hands. The gentle choreography animated the pages of the schoolbooks that still hovered in my imagination, and brought back my own father's discussions about the ancient travelers here, Herodotus and Pausanius. The old truism rings true about the thrill of history coming alive, but there was more.

Something ancient and holy was unfolding all around me. It was what the wandering pilgrim-poet Basho called "a glimpse of the under-glimmer," an experience of the deeply real that lurks everywhere beneath centuries of stereotypes and false images that prevent us from truly see-ing other people, other places, other times. An enormous gratitude welled up in me for the ritual kindness accorded the stranger. Me. During those hours I was never more a stranger and, uncannily enough, never more at home. That encounter was the first of many in my life that drove home the unsettling but inescapable fact that we are all strangers in this world and that part of the elusive wonder of travel is that during those moments far away from all that is familiar, we are forced to face that truth, which is to say, the sacred truth of our *soul's journey* here on earth. This is one reason the stranger has always been held in awe and why the stranger on the move is perpetually a soul in wonder.

Toward twilight, a stillness came over the Bedouins. The sun was setting below the long red line of the desert horizon. Silently, we watched while the tea simmered and the smell of cinnamon lingered in the air. It was a stillness that was there before the pyramids, a timelessness I hadn't known until then that I had longed for.

I felt utterly happy.

That afternoon of simple travel pleasures changed me. Farther down the road, over the next year of my travels which took me from Egypt through the Greek Islands and around Israel, Ahmet's respectful tone of voice resounded like a blessing. By naming my journey a pilgrimage, he had conferred a kind of dignity on it that altered the way I have traveled ever since. He had detected that I was at a crossroads in my life and seeking answers. With that kind of intention and intensity, my travels were moving question marks, as if journeys to ancient oracles. Each stage of my trek through the Mediterranean for the next year became imbued with the *spirit* of pilgrimage in which I was aware, as never before, of traveling back in time in search of the *sacred*, to places where the gods shined forth, to holy ground that blazed with meaning. I found it in the place I least expected, a few hundred yards away from famous tombs of Tutankhamen and Ramses VI, in the timeless shade of a Bedouin camp.

In the more than twenty years since that journey, I've traveled around the world, marveling both at its seven-times-seven thousand wonders, and at the frustration of fellow travelers I saw at those same sites, whose faces, if not their voices, cried out like the torch singer, "*Is that all there is?*"

I am haunted by the memory of an old friend who spent three days at Stonehenge, leaning against the megaliths, dreaming of Druids and King Arthur, and yet felt nothing. I remember meeting an Australian wanderer on the fifteen-mile hike through the Samaria Gorge in Crete who had been on the road for five years. He boasted of "taking in," as he put it, most of the world's monuments, then sighed the sigh of the world-weary. He hadn't really been impressed, he confessed, by any-thing, anywhere. "History is overrated," he concluded torpidly, as we reached the end of our hike. In response, he decided to live in a cave there on the beach for a few more years. I recall, too, the cruise ships I've lectured on and the passengers who never disembarked at Bali, Istanbul, Crete, or the island of Komodo, preferring to stay on board to play cards or watch old videos. Besides hearing a thousand com-plaints through the years by bored and disappointed travelers, I'm also aware of the spate of angst-ridden travel writers complaining we've gone from a world of classical ruins to sites simply ruined by too many (other) tourists.

What strikes me about all these incidents is not my fellow travel-ers' cynicism or jadedness, but the way their faces and voices and words betray the longing for something more than their travels were giving them. Conjuring up their collective disappointment, I'm reminded of the statement I read years ago in the *Irish Times* by a Connemara man after he was arrested for a car accident. "There were plenty of onlookers, but no witnesses." In other words, we may log impressive miles in our travels but see nothing; we may follow all the advice in the travel magazines and still feel little enthusiasm.

Of course, the gap between ecstasy and irony in the realm of travel is a reflection of the abyss of experience in modern life. The phenom-enon strikes at the core of this book. I don't believe that the problem is in the sites as it is in the sighting, the way we *see*. It's not simply in the images that lured us there and let us down, as in the *imagining* that is required of us. Nor does the blame lie in the faiths that inspire throngs to visit religious, artistic, and cultural monuments, as much as in our own lack of faith that we can experience anything authentic any-more.

With the roads to the exalted places we all want to visit more crowded than ever, we look more and more, but see less and less. But we don't need more gimmicks and gadgets; all we need do is *reimagine* the way we travel. If we truly want to know the secret of soulful travel, we need to believe that there is something sacred waiting to be discovered in virtually every journey.

There are as many forms of travel as there are proverbial roads to Rome. The tourism business offers comfort, predictability, and entertainment; business travel makes the world of commerce go 'round. There is exploration for the scholar and the scientist, still eager to encounter the unknown and add to the human legacy of knowledge. The centuries-old tradition of touring to add to social status endures, as does traveling to ancient sites for the sheer aesthetic "pleasure of ruins," as Rose Macaulay described it. In the seventeenth century emerged the custom of the Grand Tour, which recommended travel as the last stage of a gentleman's education. Most recent is the phenomenon of the "W.T.," the World Traveler, renowned for drifting for the sake of drifting, and the "F.B.T.," the Frequent Business Traveler.

For each of these kinds of travel, there are more resources than ever. Bookstore shelves groan under the weight of guidebooks that cover major sightseeing in more than 200 nations around the world, custom regional guides for restaurants, cruises, architecture, gardens, ballparks, homes of famous artists and authors, guides for safe travel, and even a guide to the "most dangerous places in the world."

All of these roads to Rome are legitimate for different travelers, at different stages of life. But what if we are at the crossroads, as the blues singers moan, longing for something else, neither diversion nor dis-traction, escape nor mere entertainment? What if we have finally wearied of the paladins of progress who promise worry-free travel, and long for a form of travel that responds to a genuine *cri du coeur*, a long-ing for a taste of mystery, a touch of the sacred?

For millennia, this cry in the heart for embarking upon a mean-ingful journey has been answered by pilgrimage, *a transformative jour-ney to a sacred center*. It calls for a journey to a holy site associated with gods, saints, or heroes, or to a natural setting imbued with spiritual power, or to a revered temple to seek counsel. To people the world over, pilgrimage is a spiritual exercise, an act of devotion to find a source of healing, or even to perform a penance. Always, it is a journey of risk and renewal. For a journey without challenge has no meaning; one without purpose has no soul.

Over the years, I've participated in many traditional forms of reli-gious pilgrimage, as well as modern secular ones, and trekked through the accounts of a wide range of travelers throughout history. I am con-vinced that pilgrimage is still a bona fide spirit-renewing ritual. But I also believe in pilgrimage as a powerful metaphor for *any* journey with the purpose of finding something that matters deeply to the traveler. With a deepening of focus, keen preparation, attention to the path below our feet, and respect for the destination at hand, it is possible to transform even the most ordinary trip into a sacred journey, a pilgrim-age. In the spirit of the poet John Berryman, who reserved his severest criticism for "unobserved" writing, I don't believe tourism is the prob-lem; the struggle is against unimaginative traveling. What legendary travelers have taught us since Pausanius and Marco Polo is that the art of travel is the art of seeing what is sacred.

Pilgrimage is the kind of journeying that marks just this move from mindless to mindful, soulless to soulful travel. The difference may be subtle or dramatic; by definition it is life-changing. It means being alert to the times when all that's needed is a trip to a remote place to simply *lose* yourself, and to the times when what's needed is a journey to a sacred place, in all its glorious and fearsome masks, to *find* yourself. Since the earliest human peregrinations, the nettlesome question has been: *How* do we travel more fruitfully, more wisely, more soulfully? How can we mobilize the imagination and enliven the heart so that we might, on our special journeys, "see everywhere in the world the inevitable expression of the concept of infinity," in the words of Louis Pasteur; or notice, along with Thoreau, "the divine energy everywhere"? Or recall with Evan S. Connell, Jr. the advice to medieval travelers: *Pass by that which you do not love.*

The earliest recorded pilgrimage is accorded to Abraham, who left Ur 4,000 years ago, seeking the inscrutable presence of God in the vast desert. His descendants Moses, Paul, and Mohammed embody the notion of sacred journeys. The Bible, the Torah, and the Koran, the holy texts of Hinduism and Buddhism—all admonish their followers to flock to the birthplaces and tombs of the prophets, the sites where miracles occurred, or the paths they walked in search of enlightenment.

We know of people as early as the fourth and fifth centuries leaving their villages to journey along the "glory road" to the Holy Land so that they might tread in the footsteps of Christ. By the eighth century, the first travelers were making the *hajj* to Medina and Mecca to make contact with sites made holy by the prophet Mohammed. Between the fifth and tenth centuries, the Irish made the *turas*, the circuit to the shrines of saints and ancient Celtic heroes. Besides religious pilgrimages, we have ample evidence of lovers of philosophy and poetry going to the shrines of classical writers in Athens, Ephesus, Alexandria, and to the tombs of Dante, Virgil, and the troubadours.

During the Middle Ages, going on pilgrimage to a holy site became an immensely popular practice and, in a way, was a forerunner of modern tourism. To help them on the long and often dangerous road to Jerusalem, Rome, Mecca, or Canterbury, medieval pilgrims often carried an inspirational book: a small Bible, a Book of Hours, even a literary classic such as the *Iliad* or a work by Dante. Eventually, a kind of guide-book began to appear, such as the *Marvels of Rome*, which was immensely popular for the traveler and pilgrim to the ancient sites of the city.

For the ancient pilgrimage to the tomb of Saint James at Santiago de Compostela in northwest Spain, which attracted hundreds of thousands of pilgrims every year from the eleventh to the eighteenth centuries, travelers consulted an indispensable little book, simply called *The Pilgrim's Guide*. Thought by some to have been written by Pope Callixtus, whereas others believe it was authored by a thirteenth-century Frenchman named Aimery Picaud, *The Pilgrim's Guide* combined inspiration and useful references and is now regarded as the prototype for modern guidebooks. Within its leather-bound pages were descriptions of the "sights, shrines, and people" that the traveler was likely to meet along the "pilgrim's road," along with prayers for safe journeys, lists of relics, architectural wonders, commentaries both kind and caustic about those one might encounter along the route, and a list of inns that welcomed pilgrims with complimentary meals and lodging.

In modern times, Lord Byron's *Childe Harold's Pilgrimage* was the "sacred" text for romantic poets traveling to Greece, while Mark Twain's *Innocents Abroad* served as a whimsical guidebook for the first generation of American travelers to Europe and the Holy Land. The sacred can also be exploited. On the nefarious side is the *Book of Buried Pearls and of the Precious Mystery, Giving Indications Regarding the Hiding Places of Finds and Treasures*, a manual of advice to looters, which contributed to the pillaging of Egyptian tombs.

In our time, Isak Dinesen's *Out of Africa* and Jack Kerouac's *On the Road* have stuffed the rucksacks of thousands of travelers who agree with Umberto Eco that it is "electrifying" to read about a place you've dreamed about visiting while actually there. *The Art of Pilgrimage* follows in the footsteps of the venerable "Pilgrim's Guides." It is designed for

"crossroads travelers"—those who have the deep desire to make a significant or symbolic journey and need some inspiration and a few spiritual tools for the road. It is also for those who are frequent business
travelers and holiday-makers who would like a few tips to make their
journeys more memorable. At the heart of this book is the belief that
virtually every traveler can transform any journey into pilgrimage with a
commitment to finding something personally sacred along the road.

Today, the practice of pilgrimage is enjoying a vigorous revival, perhaps more popular now than at any time since its peak during the
Middle Ages, when millions annually followed the pilgrim paths to
thousands of shrines all over Europe. As part of the celebrations for the
turning of the millennium, the Vatican has declared A.D. 2000 "The
Year of the Pilgrim." In a good tourist year, 3 to 4 million visit Rome;
50 million people are expected to descend upon Rome in 2000, to
touch the relics and tread the holy ground.

From Ireland to Romania, Greenland to Patagonia, old churches,
long in disrepair, homes of noteworthy authors and scientists, even torture chambers in St. Petersburg and Phnom Penh, are being restored or
opened to lure tourists. Enterprising guides are leading hordes of literary pilgrims along the footsteps of the Beats in Greenwich Village, the
Bloomsbury crowd in London, and the Lost Generation in Paris, so
that they might feel the thrill of association with genius. Nature
reserves in India for tigers, and in Africa for elephants, are being cor-
doned off and advertised as pilgrimages for lovers of the last bastions of
wilderness. In Los Angeles, old hearses carry the starstruck to the
hotels and seedy bars where the famous and infamous died.

Truly, the phenomenon of pilgrimage is thriving, though it never
really disappeared. Peel away the palimpsest of the glossy images of
tourism and you'll find ancient ideas. Still, the question remains as vital
as it has for centuries when pilgrims turned to priests, rabbis, sheiks,
mentors, and veterans from the venerated path: How do we *make* a pilgrimage? Turn an ordinary trip into a sacred one? How might we use

that wisdom to see more soulfully, listen more attentively, and imagine more keenly on *all* our journeys? Either while trekking to Mount Kailas, Mecca, or Memphis? Exploring a distant landscape, a famous museum, or a favorite hometown park? Are there lessons to be learned from great travelers, tasks to follow in the manner of true pilgrims, that can make sacred our travels?

Twenty-five hundred years ago, Lao Tzu said, "The longest journey begins with a single step." For those of us fascinated with the spiritual quest, the deepening of our journeys begins the moment we begin to ask what is sacred to us: architecture, history, music, books, nature, food, religious heritage, family history, the lives of saints, scholars, heroes, artists?

However, a caveat. "The point of the pilgrimage," as a Buddhist priest told the traveling author Oliver Statler on his journey around the Japanese island of Shikoku, "is to improve yourself by enduring and overcoming difficulties." In other words, if the journey you have chosen is indeed a pilgrimage, a soulful journey, it will be rigorous. Ancient wisdom suggests if you aren't trembling as you approach the sacred, it isn't the real thing. The sacred, in its various guises as holy ground, art, or knowledge, evokes emotion *and* commotion.

The Art of Pilgrimage is designed for those who intend to embark on any journey with a deep purpose but are unsure of how to prepare for it or endure it. As the title suggests, this book emphasizes the *art* of pilgrimage, which to my mind signals the skill of personally creating your own journey, and the daily practice of slowing down and lingering, savoring, and absorbing each of its stages. This is a book of reminders and resources, literally designed to encourage what Buddhists call mindfulness, and what Ray Charles calls "soulfulness"—the ability to respond from our deepest place.

The book's seven chapters follow the universal "round" of the sacred journey, exploring the ways in which the common rites of pilgrimage might inspire modern equivalents for today's traveler. Like John Bunyan's famous pilgrim, the book progresses from *The Longing* to *The Call* that beckons us onward, then the drama of *Departure*, the treading of *The Pilgrim's Way* and beyond to *The Labyrinth* and *Arrival*, before coming full circle to the challenge of *Bringing Back the Boon.*

Within these chapters are stories, anecdotes, quotes, and vignettes, interlaced with practical suggestions from travelers, artists, and pilgrims throughout history. Connecting these voices are a series of meditations or contemplations that suggest different ways to practice what pilgrims and poets and keenly perceptive travelers have done for centuries, to see with the "eyes of the heart," as the Sufis say, and transform the inevitable ordeals of your journey into opportunities to learn something about yourself and the wide world around you. Also, there are imagination exercises I have used myself in my own travels and have encouraged those who have taken my art and literary tours through such countries as Ireland, England, France, Greece, and Turkey. They are designed to move you from a dependence on others' images of the world to *imagining* how you might walk your own path to the holy ground of your heart's desire.

As the Sufi mystic Mevlana Rumi wrote seven centuries ago, "Don't be satisfied with the stories that come before you; unfold your own myth." His poetic brother here in the West, Walt Whitman, put it this way: "Not I—not anyone else, can travel that road for you. You must travel it yourself."

Together, these musings aspire to the idea echoed in the work of seekers everywhere, that travelers cannot find deep meaning in their journey until they encounter what is truly sacred. What is sacred is what is worthy of our reverence, what evokes awe and wonder in the human heart, and what when contemplated transforms us utterly.

Surely, a voice whispered to me one night in the ruins of an old castle in Donegal, Ireland, *surely there is a secret way.*

The moon was rising like a celestial mirror over the heathered hills. The sea slapped at the peculiar basalt rock formations along the coast. The wind howled like Gaelic pipes. From a distant farmhouse came the sweet smell of burning peat.

I stood shivering in the stone archway of an ancient chapel. Turning my head, I saw the weathered carving of a centuries-old Knot of Eternity. Each thread wandered far from the center, then whorled back in again. The ancient Celts believed this to be a potent symbol of life's journey, and the desire to return to the source that replenishes the soul.

Slowly, I followed the old stone path with my finger. Around and around went my hand, feeling the ancient chisel marks, the abrasions of wind, rain, and sun, and the tender burnishing of time. I thought of all the travelers who had come there, step by step, prayer by prayer, and wondered if they had discovered what they had been seeking, if their faith had been restored.

Slowly, the moon lit the ancient stone. The night air stung my eyes. My hand kept moving across the eternal knot, seeking out the hidden pattern beneath the whorling stone.

In that sublime moment I felt an ancient presence rise in my heart, and in my fingertips the unwinding spiral of joy.

This is the path that *The Art of Pilgrimage* follows, one carved out by the simple beauty of a handful of practices, tasks, and exercises that pilgrims, sojourners, and explorers of all kinds have used for millennia. In each of us dwells a wanderer, a gypsy, a pilgrim. The purpose here is to call forth that spirit. What matters most on your journey is how deeply you see, how attentively you hear, how richly the encounters are felt in your heart and soul.

Kabir wrote, "If you have not experienced something for yourself, then for it is not real." So it is with pilgrimage, which is the art of movement, the poetry of motion, the music of personal experience of the sacred in those places where it has been known to shine forth. If we are not astounded by these possibilities, we can never plumb the depths of our own souls or the soul of the world.

Hearing this, let the voyage begin, recalling the words of the Spanish poet Antonio Machado:

> *Traveler, there is no path*
> *paths are made by walking.*

Phil Cousineau
San Francisco, California
April 1998

I
THE LONGING

For in their hearts doth Nature stir them so,
Then people long on pilgrimage to go,
And palmers to be seeking foreign strands,
To distant shrines renowned in sundry lands.

—Geoffrey Chaucer,
The Canterbury Tales

N February 1996, together with my brother Paul, I took the long boat ride up the Mekong River in Cambodia to see one of the great riddles of the ancient world, the sacred sprawl of ruined temples and palaces that a twelfth-century traveler said "housed numerous marvels."

On our first morning at the walled city of Angkor Wat, we witnessed a glorious sunrise over its lotus-crowned towers, then began the ritual walk up the long bridgeway toward the sanctuary. Our arms were draped across each other's shoulders. Our heads shook at the impossibly beautiful sight of the "marvelous enigma" that early European chroniclers regarded as one of the Wonders of the World, and later colonialists described as rivaling the divinely inspired architecture of Solomon.

We walked as if in a fever-dream. Halfway down the causeway, we paused to take in the beauty of the shifting light. We snapped a few photographs of the *nagas*, the five-headed stone serpents, that undulated along the moat and of the chiseled lacework in the colossal gateway looming before us, then grinned at each other and took a deep breath of the morning air. At that moment, we noticed a gray-robed Buddhist nun limping by us on her way to the temple. Her head was shaved and bronzed. When she drew even with us, I held out an offering, which she calmly accepted with stumps where once had been hands. Stunned, I then realized why she had been walking as if on stilts. Her feet had been severed at the ankle and she was hobbling on the knobs of her ankles. I was stricken with images of her mutilation by the demonic Khmer Rouge, then wondered if she'd been a victim of one of the 11 million landmines forgotten in the forests, fields, and roads of Cambodia.

Her eyes met mine with a gaze of almost surreal serenity. Utterly moved, we offered a few dollars for the shrine in the temple. She calmly accepted the donation in a small woven bag, bowed, and limped away, like a thin-legged crane moving stiffly through the mud of one of the nearby ponds.

The encounter with the Cambodian nun was an ominous way to begin our visit, a gift briefly disguised as a disturbance. Her enigmatic smile eerily anticipated the expression on the sculptured faces of the fifty-four giant bodhisattvas that loomed in the Holy of Holies above the nearby pyramid temples of the Bayon. Each time I met their timeless gaze, my heart leapt. As the lotus ponds and pools throughout the complex were created to reflect each work of religious art, the faces of the bodhisattvas and the nun mirrored each other. I began to think of the nun as the embodiment of the Bodhisattva Avalokiteshvara,

A Buddhist nun sits next to the lacework reliefs of the Bayon temple at Angkor Thom, selling incense and candles to pilgrims who have come to pray.

the god of inexhaustible compassion, who has come to symbolize the miracle of Angkor for millions of pilgrims.

How far does your forgiveness reach? the sculpted faces ask from a thousand statues.

As far as prayers allow, the nun's eyes seemed to respond.

I rambled through the ruins with my brother for the next several hours, stunned by our sheer good fortune of being there. The Angkor complex was destroyed in the fifteenth century, then forgotten for 400 years and overrun with the stone-strangling vines of the jungle. Marveling at the beauty laced with terror in the stories of our young Cambodian guide (who told us the local villagers believed that Angkor was built by angels and giants), time seemed poised on the still-point of the world. This was more than an architectural curiosity, a pious parable of fleeting glory; it was a microcosm of the universe itself. According to scholars, the walls, moats, and soaring terraces represented the different levels of existence itself. The five towers of Angkor symbolized the five peaks of Mount Meru, the center of the world in Hindu cosmology. This was the world mountain in stone, a monumental mandala encompassed by moats that evoked the oceans. A visit was an accomplishment demanding the rigorous climbing of precipitously steep staircases, built that way not without reason.

"It is clear," wrote Vice Admiral Bonard, an early colonialist, "that the worshiper penetrating the temple was intended to have a tangible sense of moving to higher and higher levels of initiation." Our three days stretched on. The hours seemed to contain days, the days held weeks, as in all dreamtime adventures. We were graced with one strangely moving encounter after another. Silently, we mingled with saffron-robed monks who had walked hundreds of miles in the footsteps of their ancestors from Cambodia, Thailand, India, and Japan to pray in the sanctuary of a place believed for a thousand years to be the center of the world. Gratefully, we traded road stories with travelers who'd been through Burma, Vietnam, and China. After dark, we read the accounts of fellow pilgrims who had been making the arduous trek here by foot for centuries, from China and Japan in ancient times, then by car from France and England, and by boat from America.

Though neither Buddhist nor Hindu, wandering through the site I was more than smitten by the romancing of old stones. In the uncanny way of spiritually magnetized centers of pilgrimage, I felt a wonderful calm exploring the derelict pavilions, abandoned libraries, and looted monasteries. My imagination was animated by the strange and wonderful challenge to fill in what time had destroyed, thrilling to the knowledge that tigers, panthers, and elephants still roamed over the flagstones of these shrines when Angkor was rediscovered in the 1860s.

But through our visit the dark thread ran.

With every step through the ghostly glory of the ancient temple grounds, it was impossible not to be reminded of the scourge of Pol Pot, the ever-present threat of landmines, and the fragility of a site that had endured a thousand years of historical chaos. The maimed children and fierce soldiers we encountered everywhere were grim evidence of a never-ending war. Once upon a time, foreigners were spared the horrors of remote revolutions, but no more. In a local English-language newspaper, we read that Pol Pot had ordered the executions of three Australian tourists, saying only, "Crush them."

Overshadowing even this were the twinges of guilt I felt for having undertaken the journey—Jo, my partner back in San Francisco, was seven months pregnant with our baby. Though she was selflessly supportive, I was uneasy. So why make such a risky journey?

To fulfill a vow.

Twice in the previous fifteen years, my plans to make the long trek to the ruins of Angkor had been thwarted at the Thai-Cambodia border. Dreading that war might break out again and the borders clamp shut for another twenty years, I believed that the research trip my brother and I were on in the Philippines serendipitously offered a last chance to fulfill a promise to my father.

On my eleventh birthday, he had presented me with a book, not a Zane Grey Western or the biography of my hometown baseball hero, Al Kaline, that I had asked for, but a book with a bronze-tinted cover depicting sculptures of fabulous creatures from a distant world. These creatures were not from a phantasmagorical planet out of science fiction, but the long-forgotten world of the Khmers, the ancient civilization that had built Angkor.

From that moment on, the book came to symbolize for me the hidden beauty of the world. With the transportive magic that only books possess, it offered a vision of the vast world outside of my small hometown in Michigan; it set a fire in my heart and through the years inspired in me the pilgrim's desire to see this wondrous place for myself.

When my father became ill in the fall of 1984, I drove cross-country from San Francisco to Detroit to see him and, in an effort to lift his spirits, promised him that when he recovered we would travel together. I tried to convince him that after years of unfulfilled plans to see Europe, we would travel together to Amsterdam and visit Van Gogh's nephew, whom he had once guided on a personal tour through Ford's River Rouge complex in Dearborn. After Holland, I suggested, we could take the train to Périgueux in southern France and track down the story of our ancestors who had left there in 1678. Then, I said haltingly, we could take a direct flight from Paris to Phnom Penh and visit Angkor Wat. He seemed pleased by the former, puzzled by the latter.

"Don't you remember the book you gave me as a boy?" I asked him, disappointed in his response to my cue. "The one on the excavations at Angkor?" He riffled through the memory of a lifetime of books he had bestowed on friends and family. Then his face lit up, and he harrumphed, "Oh, yes. *Angkor*, the Malcolm MacDonald book, the one with the sculptures of the Terrace of the Leper King on the cover." He paused to consider the possibilities of our traveling together, then painfully readjusted himself in his old leather reading chair.

The recently restored sculpture and walls of the Terrace of the Leper King, built by Yasovarman, founder of Angkor Wat.

"I just wish I were as confident as you that I was going to recover," he said with the first note of despair I'd ever heard from him. "Of course, I'd like to see these places with you. It would be *wonderful.*" Then his voice broke. "But I don't know, son, if I'm going to make it."

No one I've ever met has pronounced the word "wonderful" like my father. He stressed the first syllable, "won," as if the adjective did indeed have its roots in victory and triumph. He so rarely used upbeat words, so when he did I knew he meant it. Hearing it there and then, watching this once-ferocious and formidable man sit in a chair, unable to move his hands and feet because of a crippling nerve disease, I was shaken. Still, I feigned confidence and courage and promised we would hit the road together as soon as he recovered.

He didn't. Four months later, on the very Ides of March which he had announced every year in our house as though it were the strangest day on the calendar, my father died in his sleep.

Shortly after the funeral, while packing up the books in his stilled apartment, I made one of the few vows in my life. I promised myself I would take the journey for both of us, make the pilgrimage to a place made holy by the play of light on stone and the devotion of pilgrims who had walked astonishing distances so that they might touch the sacred sculpture and offer their prayers on the wings of incense.

And, in so doing, perhaps restore my faith in life itself.

THE ART OF PILGRIMAGE

We journey across the days as over a stone the waves.
—Paul Valéry

A ll our journeys are rhapsodies on the theme of discovery. We travel as seekers after answers we cannot find at home, and soon find that a change of climate is easier than a change of heart. The bittersweet truth about travel is embedded in the word, which derives from the older word *travail*, itself rooted in the Latin *tripalium*, a medieval torture rack. As many a far-ranging roamer has suspected, there are moments in travel that are like being "on the rack." For the wandering Bedouins, "Travel is travail." The ancient Greeks taught that obstacles were the tests of the gods, and the medieval Japanese believed that the sorrows of travel were challenges to overcome and transform into poetry and song. Whether we are on vacation, a business trip, or a far-flung adventure tour, we can look at the trying times along the road as either torment or chances to "stretch" ourselves.

But what do we do if we feel a need for something more out of our journeys than the perennial challenges and pleasures of travel? What happens if the search for the new is no longer enough? What if our heart aches for a kind of journey that defies explanation?

Centuries of travel lore suggest that when we no longer know where to turn, our real journey has just begun. At that crossroads moment, a voice calls to our pilgrim soul. The time has come to set out for the sacred ground—the mountain, the temple, the ancestral home—that will stir our heart and restore our sense of wonder. It is down the path to the deeply real where time stops and we are seized by the mysteries. This is the journey we cannot not take.

On that long and winding road, it is easy to lose the way. Listen. The old hermit along the side of the road whispers, *Stranger, pass by that which you do not love.*

"I left Tangier, my birthplace, the 13th of June, 1325," wrote Ibn Battua, one of the most remarkable spiritual seekers who ever ventured down the long and winding roads of the world, "being at the time twenty-two years of age, with the intention of making the Pilgrimage

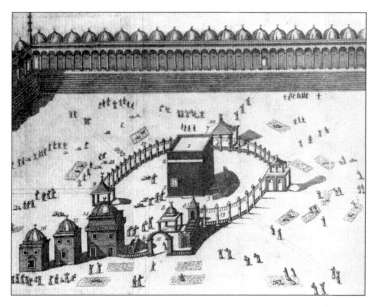

*A nineteenth-century drawing of the Mosque at Mecca, revealing hajji,
pilgrims, prostrating themselves and circumambulating the Ka'aba.*

to the Holy House [at Mecca] and the Tomb of the Prophet [at
Medina]. I set out alone, finding no companions to cheer the way with
friendly intercourse, and no party of travelers with whom to associate
myself. Swayed by an overwhelming impulse within me, and a long-
cherished desire to visit all those glorious sanctuaries, I resolved to
leave all my friends both female and male, to abandon my home as
birds abandon the nest."

For twenty-nine years, Battua made pilgrimages from Spain to
China, roaming 75,000 miles, three times the distance covered by
Marco Polo. When he finally returned to Morocco, he wrote in his
astonishing *rihla*, or travel book, that his native land was "the best of
countries, for its fruits are plentiful, and running water and nourishing
food are never exhausted."

If it is so that one's home is the "best of countries," why do millions of us, every year since time immemorial, cast our fates to the wind and follow the ancient tracks of the pilgrim roads of the world? By what "overwhelming impulse" are we swayed to travel to faraway places at great cost and often at great risk?

For Ibn Battua, the longing was a chorus of calls: religious, scientific, poetic, political, and mercenary. He was the quintessential pilgrim, spiritually grounded, soulfully inspired, responding to what Goethe called "the holy longing," the desire to be caught up in a deeper quest.

Meanwhile, according to the German scholar of travel, Winfried Löschburg, "the longing to defeat distance, the longing for the unknown became stronger and stronger in parts of Europe. It was the desire to escape the baronial castle or the convent-school, and move out into the wide world through the town gates...." Anatole France wrote that during the Age of Exploration, the urge was described as *un long desire*, the passionate pursuit of the hidden or forbidden, the novel or the legendary; impossible to satisfy but equally impossible to ignore.

The impulse to travel is as old as stone, as timeless as the rising and setting of the sun. Zora Neale Hurston felt that "Travel is the soul of civilization." To some, the urge is for motion itself, as with Robert Louis Stevenson, who wrote, "For my part I travel not to go anywhere, but to go. I travel for travel's sake. The great affair is to move." The very word *traveler* conjures up images of the romance of movement. Henry David Thoreau wrote, "A traveler. I love his title. A traveler is to be reverenced as such. His profession is the best symbol of our life. Going from—toward; it is the history of every one of us."

To others, like the French novelist Colette, travel suggests sensuous possibilities: "I am going away with him to an unknown country where I shall have no past and no name, and where I shall be born again with a new face and an untried heart." To the rapscallion rover Mark Twain, long journeys held out the possibility of self-improvement: "Travel is

The mere glimpse of exotic passport stamps is enough to ignite wanderlust in the heart of the true traveler.

fatal to prejudice, bigotry, and narrow-mindedness." The nomadic Bruce Chatwin told how a tramp once described his own compulsion to wander: "It's as though the tides was pulling you along the high road." In her landmark anthology *Maiden Voyages*, Mary Morris cites Lawrence Durrell's splendid description of Freya Stark as an example of the way women "move differently through the world." Durrell writes, "A great traveler . . . is a kind of introspective; as she covers the ground outwardly, so she advances fresh interpretations of herself inwardly."

There is a tradition of travel as a kind of peripatetic university. In his classic book *Abroad*, Paul Fussell writes, "Before the development of tourism, travel was conceived to be like study, and its fruits were considered to be the adornment of the mind and the formation of judgment. The traveler was a student of what he sought. . . ." But, Fussell postulates, the romantic aura and aristocratic associations surrounding travel changed irrevocably with the humbling horrors of World War I. Now there is no more true exploration, no serious travel, only "jet travel to ruins."

Thus the paradox: The easier it becomes to travel widely, on the wings of supersonic jets and via the Internet, the harder it becomes to travel *wisely*. We are left with plenty of frequent-flier miles and passport stamps, but the gnawing suspicion grows that our travels lack something vital. T. S. Eliot was driven to ask of the modern age,

Where is the wisdom we have lost in knowledge?
Where is the knowledge we have lost in information?

Imagine your first memorable journey. What images rise up in your soul? They may be of a childhood visit to the family gravesite, the lecture your uncle gave at a famous battlefield, or the hand-in-hand trip with your mother to a religious site. What feelings are evoked by your enshrined travel memories? Do they have any connection with your life today? Have you ever made a vow to go someplace that is sacred to you, your family, your group? Have you ever *imagined* yourself in a place that stirred your soul like the song of doves at dawn?

If not you, then who? If not now, when? If not here, where? Paris? Benares? Memphis?

Uncover what you long for and you will discover who you are.

THE TRAVELER WHO IS
TAKEN SERIOUSLY

Pilgrims are poets who create
by taking journeys.
—Richard R. Niebuhr

According to the dictionary, the word *pilgrimage* derives from the Latin *peligrinus*, foreigner or wayfarer, the journey of a person who travels to a shrine or holy place. Another older derivation, more poetic, reveals that *pilgrim* has its roots in the Latin *per agrum*, "through the field." This ancient image suggests a curious soul who walks beyond known boundaries, crosses fields, touching the earth

A nineteenth-century postcard found in an old bookstall along the Seine River in Paris, showing a "Wandering Bohemian," as the bouquiniste, *or bookseller, described it.*

with a destination in mind and a pur-pose in heart. This pilgrim is a way-farer who longs to endure a difficult journey to reach the sacred center of his or her world, a place made holy by a saint, hero, or god. Once there, the desire is to touch a relic, have a vision, hear an oracle, and to experi-ence what psychologist Stephen Larsen calls the "irruption of the divine in a three-dimensional place." In Richard R. Niebuhr's elegant description,

Pilgrims are persons in motion— passing through territories not their own—seeking something we might call completion, or perhaps the word clarity will do as well, a goal to which only the spirit's compass points the way.

Traditional pilgrims such as Abraham, Basho, Saint Jerome, Saint Egeria, Chaucer, and Dante—and their modern counterparts William Least Heat Moon, Freya Stark, Isabelle Eberhardt, Sir Richard Burton, Thomas Merton, Paulo Coelho's young pilgrim on the Old Path to Santiago de Compostela, Ray Kinsella in the baseball movie *Field of Dreams*, or Isak Dinesen in *Out of Africa*—all have left chronicles of their journeys. From them we can discern a few telltale patterns.

The pilgrim's motives have always been manifold: to pay homage, to fulfill a vow or obligation, to do penance, to be rejuvenated spiritu-ally, or to feel the release of catharsis. The journeys all begin in a restive state, in deep disturbance. Something vital was missing in life: Vitality itself may be lurking on the road or at the heart of a distant sanctuary.

The ritual act of pilgrimage attempts to fill that emptiness. It can happen halfway around the world, as it did with a very kind priest I know—Father Theodore Walters of Toledo, Ohio, who began leading groups to the Marian Shrine at Medjugorje, Yugoslavia, because he believed that modern people desperately needed "a healing vision from the Mother of God." He also confessed that he believed a war-battered country might need the kindness people on pilgrimage convey from the sheer gratitude brimming in their hearts.

Pilgrimage can also occur just down the road, as it did to a married couple I met briefly, who had reached an impasse in their creative endeavors. They said they had lost their voice and needed "to hear the voice of commitment to words again." In response, they decided to reinvigorate their love of literature by traveling to the poet Robinson Jeffers' stone house in Carmel, California. My old friend Michael Jajuga was under so much stress during medical school that once a month he would rejuvenate himself with what he called his "nature pilgrimages." He would drive all night in his 1970 Challenger into the woods of northern Michigan so he could go trout fishing for a few hours before returning home. That brief contact was his "golden time," he used to say—his sacred time.

Participation can be communal, as was scholar China Galland's march with a million other pilgrims to the Shrine of Our Lady of Czestochowa in Jasna Gora Monastery, Poland. Or it may be solitary, as with the World War II pilot I met in Tokyo in the mid-1980s, who had just returned from a sorrowful visit to ground zero in Hiroshima.

What unites the different forms of pilgrimage is intensity of intention, the soul's desire to respond to return to the center, whether it portends ecstasy or agony. What makes a pilgrimage sacred is the longing behind the journey, reminiscent of the famous sixteenth-century

"The Spiritual Pilgrim." The French astronomer Camille
Flammarion adapted this image from a sixteenth-century
German woodcut.

woodcut of the *Pilgrim Astronomer,* who pokes his head through a slit in
the dome of the sky so that he might gaze at the machinery behind the
sun, stars, and moon and so unveil the mystery of creation.

WHAT IS MISSING LONGS
TO BE FILLED IN

We thirst at first.
—Emily Dickinson

Emily Dickinson knew well the tidal pulls of creative desire. She
made daily pilgrimages to sacred places in her imagination, renew-
ing herself with each recognition of her creative needs. Thirst, hunger,

Legendary bibliophile George Whitman (inset) at the helm of his Shakespeare and Company Bookstore in Paris. At right, a photo of the bookstore, circa 1950s.

the yearning for touch—the metaphors are countless. Thoreau suggests that the longing may be the stirrings of remorse that we are not living up to our potential: "We do not commonly live our life out and full; we do not fill all our pores with our blood; we do not inspire and expire fully and entirely enough.... We live but a fraction of our life. Why do we not let on the flood, raise the gates, and set all our wheels in motion?"

Pilgrims have reached this crossroads. Suddenly, it is important for them to see for themselves, to set foot on, to touch, to listen to the presence in the sanctuary, whether it's the Blue Mosque in Istanbul or the Shakespeare and Company Bookstore in Paris. Contact with the ground and contact with the relics at the end of the journey means getting in touch with the holy ground that spurs our faith onward.

To be touched, we must, in turn, touch. When life has lost its meaning, a pilgrim will risk everything to get back *in touch* with life. This is why relics, such as a tooth of the Buddha, the dried blood of Christ, or a Shakespeare folio, are objects that must be touched as an integral part of the pilgrimage. This is what the risk is for, the *confirmation* that the mystery exists at all in a modern world seemingly determined to undermine the sacred as mere superstition. Every day, we can read articles "exposing" ancient mysteries—the soul is "nothing but the electrical firing of synapses in the brain," dreams are the result only of "chemical combustion in the mind," love is simply the blind attraction of two incompetent personalities. Worse yet, it is now bandied about that the miracle of life itself is but a chance occurrence, a universal hiccup.

The pilgrim mood is aroused. The idea that redwood groves, an eagle's eyesight, the formation of coral, the grip of a baby's hand, the Bach suites, the echo of God in the poetry of Sappho and Pablo Neruda are all but a burp of evolution makes the soul recoil and long for a journey to reconfirm the *presence* behind sacred mysteries.

The desire for the deeply real at sacred sites around the world is what prompts intrepid souls to set out on long journeys to Rome, Jerusalem, Mecca, Ayers Rock, Medicine Wheel, Glastonbury, Croagh Patrick, Thingvellir, Macchu Pichu, Canterbury, Stratford-on-Avon, Walden, and their secular counterparts, the Field of Dreams in Iowa, or the home of the Brönte sisters in Yorkshire.

To William Melczer, an authority on the Santiago de Compostela pilgrimage, the "deeper effect" of treading the ancient track was "regeneration" and "self-purification." In *The Songlines*, Bruce Chatwin writes, "There was an idea in the Middle Ages, that by going on pilgrimage, as Muslim pilgrims do, you were reinstating the original condition of man. The act of walking through a wilderness was thought to bring you back to God." On the heels of that idea, Löschburg writes, "The most important journey for the people of the Middle Ages was the

The ruins of Glastonbury Abbey, Glastonbury, England, a sacred pilgrimage point for visits to the Chalic Well. Underneath this magnificent archway is the legendary burial place of King Arthur and Lady Guinevere.

pilgrimage. Thousands of clerics and laymen, men and women, the rich and the poor from all countries of Europe, went to Jerusalem, to Rome, to Loreto in the center of Italy, or Santiago de Compostela in northwest Spain, a mighty and constant movement of people. Soon the church could speak of an epidemic of pilgrimages, a plague which had to be arrested. Pilgrimages usually imposed for doing penitence, as often as not became a cover for the longing to travel, for adventure and for fulfilling the desire to see the fabled East; in some way a form of medieval tourism."

These are the pulls a soul feels once or twice in a lifetime. When asked about these matters of destiny, Laurens van der Post described how the Bushmen distinguished the two hungers in human beings. The first is the hunger of the body for food; the second, and more important, is the hunger of the spirit for meaning.

"Meaning transfigures all," van der Post concluded at the end of his life.

THE ROADS OF LONGING

If you stand, stand.
If you sit, sit.
But don't wobble!
—Zen Master Ummon

On the Japanese island of Shikoku there is a thousand-year-old tradition of walking the circuit of eighty-eight shrines. Oliver Statler writes in *Japanese Pilgrimage*, "Having created the charismatic figure of the Daishi, a savior who descends from Koya to walk as a pilgrim, it was natural that the holy men should urge the people to follow in his footsteps. First they promoted pilgrimage to Koya, where he rested. Then they advocated pilgrimage to Shikoku, where he was born, where he came many times as a young monk searching for the right way, where he achieved enlightenment. Eventually they shaped a pilgrimage that went all around the island."

This concise description illuminates the plot of the pilgrimage, so to speak. But what truly gives Statler's book such power is the unfolding of what Ralph Waldo Emerson called "the undersong," the emotional current that carries us along through the very life of our inner world. "Of one thing I am certain," Statler wrote upon completing his pilgrimage,: "the transformation I yearn for is incomplete. I do not know whether I am any closer to enlightenment—I do not really expect to achieve it—but I know that the attempt is worth the effort." His yearning is both the beginning and ending of the story, both the push and pull of his journey.

In describing one of the urges towards the de rigueur Grand Tour for the eighteenth-century English gentleman, Anthony Burgess writes that the longing for the Continent stemmed from the "suspicion that you have missed the chance to do something bold and different. . . ." Richard Ford writes in his novel *Independence Day* about a real estate agent in midlife crisis whose "life has swerved badly." His driving ambition is to guide his son to several halls of fame around America, ending up at the one for baseball in Cooperstown, New York. The desperate plan is for more than a mere vacation: He hopes to heal his life and the rift with his family. "Paul and I," writes Ford, "fit in well with the pilgrim feel of things temporal—nonworshipful, nonpious, camera-toting dads and sons, dads and daughters, in summery togs, winding our certain but vaguely embarrassed way toward the Hall of Fame (as if there were something shameful about going)."

For seventeen years, the Russian-American author Joseph Brodsky returned to Venice, his "version of Paradise." Again and again, he made the foray so that he might tread the ground of his first visit when he was introduced to the mysteries of the city by an enigmatic

"Ariadne" and her "fragrant thread" of perfume. He also wanted to carry on a long "meditation on the relationship between water and land, light and dark, present and past, stone and flesh, desire and fulfillment."

In his gauzy book *Watermarks*, Brodsky writes, "Let me reiterate, water equals time and provides beauty with its double.... By rubbing water, this city improves time's looks, beautifies the future. That's what the role of this city in the universe is. Because the city is static while we are moving. The tear is proof of that. Because we go and beauty stays. Because we are headed for the future, while beauty is the eternal present."

In Brodsky's meditations, I find a model for a simple but elegant response to one of the deepest longings in us, the need for sacred beauty. His longing to see beneath the superficial beauty of Venice until he could finally and truly *see* it, moves me deeply. But Brodsky warns that questing too earnestly is an error; beauty is a "by-product of ordinary things."

We can only discover the real thing through deep observation, by the slow accretion of details.

Imagine taking seventeen years to see a place until you truly *see* it. Have you ever longed to explore a place that thoroughly? Have you yearned to find what is hidden in a site you have dreamed about, whether it is halfway around the world or halfway down the block?

Recall that Prague-born poet Rainer Maria Rilke was secretary to the sculptor Auguste Rodin and that he temporarily lost the ability to write. To Rodin, that meant that Rilke had stopping *seeing*. He suggested that the poet go to the Paris Zoo every day and look at one animal until he *saw* it. Seventy-two poems later, all about a panther, Rilke could say, as he later said of the painter Paul Cézanne, "Suddenly one has the right eyes."

Integral to the art of travel is the longing to break away from the stultifying habits of our lives at home, and to break away for however long it takes to once again truly *see* the world around us. This is why "imagination is more important than knowledge," as Albert Einstein noted, and why the art of pilgrimage is the art of reimagining how we walk, talk, listen, see, hear, write, and draw as we ready for the journey of our soul's deep desire.

Try and see your next journey as more than an itinerary, to see it rather as the "slow accretion of details." The truth of a journey is there in the strange new voices, the alluring spices in the market you never knew existed, the thrilling moment when your longing is finally fulfilled.

THE TRAVELER'S LAMP

Be ye lamps unto yourselves.
—Gautama Buddha

For centuries, the devout pilgrims who slowly circled the island of Shikoku in honor of the Japanese saint Kobo Daishi stayed in simple inns along the road. Besides food and shelter, the pilgrims were given a traveler's lamp. The pathways around the mountain villages were often treacherously wet and unstable. The portable lantern lit the way through the dark toward the warmth of the pilgrim's inn.

I've thought of this elemental image of illuminating the darkness for many years. Lanterns are among my fondest travel memories. Hurricane lamps were common on camping trips with friends in northern Michigan. My friend George Whitman, owner of Shakespeare and Company Bookstore in Paris (which was built on the site of an old monastery), tells me that lamplighting was a venerable tradition there for centuries, the honor going to "the most eccentric monk." "People long for the light," he says, "and that's what the books in my store do. They shed light in a time of darkness. That's why a bookstore is the place where heaven and earth meet."

The image utmost in my mind's eye is the brass lantern handed out by the nuns at a remote hostelry in the village of Sagada in northern Luzon, Philippines. At the time of my first visit, there was no electricity; nighttime was utter darkness. To venture anywhere in the hostel or outdoors necessitated carrying a bright and broad light. I was seized by a shuddering notion to explore the dark valley at night by lanternlight. In my hand, it felt like one of the lamps of marvels from the *Arabian Nights*.

The traveler's lamp is also an illuminating metaphor for the light that shines forth from the wisdom of travelers who have walked the path before us.

Imagine lighting an old brass lantern. Visualize the light that pours forth over the road in front of you. Can you say, as Isak Dinesen did of her home in Africa, that "This is where I ought to be"? Do you feel a longing to be somewhere else?

Think of the ways that questions illuminate the world around us. Questions tune the soul. The purpose behind questions is to initiate the quest.

Recall the words of Alan Jones, dean of Grace Cathedral in San Francisco, who writes, "We are impoverished in our longing and devoid of imagination when it comes to our reaching out to others.... We need to be introduced to our longings, because they guard our mystery."

Ask yourself what mystery is being guarded by your longing. Are you taking the time to find out? The time for this never appears; it is discovered.

THAT WHICH YOU
ARE LOOKING FOR MAY
BE CALLING YOU TO SEEK

Seek patiently and you will find.
—traditional advice of the Muses

R eading old travel books or novels set in faraway places, spinning globes, unfolding maps, playing world music, eating in ethnic restaurants, meeting friends in cafés whose walls hold the soul-talk of decades—all these things are part of never-ending travel practice, not unlike doing scales on a piano, shooting free throws, or meditating. They are exercises that help lure the longing out of the soul and honor the brooding-over of unhatched ideas for journeys.

But the oldest practice is still the best. Take your soul for a stroll. Long walks, short walks, morning walks, evening walks—whatever form or length it takes. Walking is the best way to get out of your head. Recall the invocation of the philosopher Søren Kierkegaard, who said, "Above all, do not lose your desire to walk: Every day I walk myself into a state of well-being and walk away from every illness; I have walked myself into my best thoughts." As if in his footsteps, Friedrich Nietzsche also remarked, "Never trust a thought that didn't come by walking."

THE TASK OF TASKS

This longing you express is the return message.
—Mevlana Rumi

C arl Jung wrote about his midlife crisis in his memoirs, in which he asked himself which myth he was living by. He discovered to his horror that he didn't know. "So I made it the task of tasks of my life to find out." He did this in a fascinating way, returning to a childhood fascination with building sandcastles. Intuitively, he knew that by going back to his origins, his earliest display of genuine play and imagination, he could reconstruct his life, find a pattern for what became his life story.

When poet Donald Hall met with sculptor Henry Moore, he dared to ask if Moore believed that there was a secret to life. The response astonishes: "The secret of life," Moore answered without flinching, "is to have a task, something you devote your entire life to, something you bring everything to, every minute of the day for your whole life. And the most important thing is—*it must be something you cannot possibly do.*"

Imagine the courage behind these tasks. By what sacred story are you living? What task have you set for yourself? Can you tell your life story, accomplish your task, from where you are?

If you're uncertain, turn over in your mind philosopher Alfred North Whitehead's reflection that "religion is what we do with our solitude."

Where your heart wanders during those chambered moments will show you the direction of your true longing. We speak of God and geniuses and heroes and sacred sites, but these are only names for the ineffable mystery of the force behind something our souls long to be in touch with. No practical philosophy explains this urge. It is a force from the mysterious shadow world that may in turn long for us.

"Isn't it time," Alan Jones asks, "that your drifting was consecrated into pilgrimage? You have a mission. You are needed. The road that leads to nowhere has to be abandoned. . . . It is a road for joyful pilgrims intent on the recovery of passion."

But can we ever know what our mission is? There is no one answer for everyone, but for four thousand years it has proved helpful to dwell for a moment on this thought from the *Brihaduranyaha Upanishad,* "You are what your deep driving desire is."

In travel, art, religion, and poetry, the experience and the source of the sacred is similar because, as Octavio Paz has written, "it springs from the same source. That source is *desire.* Profound desire to be other than what one seems to be."

This is otherwise known as wrestling with fate and destiny.

THE END, THE BEGINNING

The necessary thing is great, inner solitude.
What goes on inwardly is worthy of your love.
—Rainer Maria Rilke

Inward seeking, as Walker Percy has written, "is what anyone would undertake if he were not sunk in the everydayness of his own life. To become aware of the possibility of the search is to be onto something. Not to be onto something is to be in despair."

What I hear in this train-whistle prose is the melancholic side of the questing spirit. The blue wave that overcomes us, the knotting in the ribcage is a signal that we have reached an impasse. How to adequately respond to this? The first step is to treat the melancholy as a force to be followed into its depths.

In some cases, the longing may be from an entire community. In February 1998, Saint Francis Church in San Francisco's North Beach neighborhood, built for miners during the 1849 Gold Rush, reopened after a four-year closure. How had the archbishop been convinced to turn back time? According to the Reverend Stephen Gross, the notion of resurrecting the church as a shrine for pilgrimage was the clinching argument. "People from Europe used to come by the church and ask us, 'Don't Americans have shrines? Don't they make pilgrimages?' We realized that many people want something *more* out of their travels and even their everyday worship. There seems to be a longing in the world for rituals that can *lead* you to some healing. There's no quick fix, but there is the peace that a pilgrimage stop can offer. Then you just have to pray."

When asked what it was like to see the ritual unveiling of the relic of the patron saint of animals and peace, Father Stephen was obviously moved. "I get teary-eyed just thinking about that moment. Being a Franciscan, I think of how Francis longed for something significant to do with his life, and when he found it he also discovered a gift for others for all these centuries. The chance to be a light for others. So here at the new shrine we hope to embody his [Saint Francis'] spirit of peace. We hope this will be a pilgrimage destination for all those longing for peace in the world."

For environmentalist John Borton, the longing for pilgrimage wasn't to a traditional religious site, but a fundamental one, the place or places that might answer for him the inscrutable story of his family history. His wasn't a passing interest but a deep longing for clarity about his origins. He is haunted by the uncertainty of where his ancestors came from, what they endured to make a life in the New World, and what, if any, influence their lives had on him. He was convinced that it was impossible for him to move on any further with his own life until he answered these questions to his own satisfaction.

"*Continuity* is the word that comes to mind," he explains. "An overwhelming need to resolve all those fragmented images about who my sisters and I might be capable of being, based on the conflicting family history stories and the relatives we met, integrated with who we felt we were and who we wanted to be, based on our perceptions and values. We felt 'out of phase' with our lives from early childhood. We thought the quest for family history information might help us to sift the hopes, dreams, pain, and scripts of others in the past from our essence, so that we could see who we were more clearly and choose rather than react about our future."

In *The Mythic Image*, mythologist Joseph Campbell writes of "the idea of a sacred place where the walls and laws of the temporal world may dissolve to reveal a wonder apparently as old as the human race." Belief in such a place, a holy temple, a sacred mesa, or an archive of sacred knowledge, inspires hope in the pilgrim's soul; an encounter there transfigures it. The prospect stirs the soul, demands a leap of faith, and awakens joy at the crossroads. If taken in this spirit, pilgrimage is poetry in motion, a winding road to meaning.

"When your ship, long moored in harbour, gives you the illusion of being a house . . . put out to sea!" writes Brazilian archbishop Helder Camara, "save your boat's journeying soul, and your own pilgrim soul, cost what it may."

Describing this languid moment in which our world *strangifies* with sudden possibility, the French poet Jules Supervielle writes in his poem, *The Call:*

And it was then that in the depths of sleep
Someone breathed to me: "You alone can do it,
Come immediately."

II

THE CALL

Yet the Lord pleads with you still: Ask where the good road is,
the godly paths you used to walk in, in the days of long ago.
Travel there, and you will find rest for your souls.

—Jeremiah 6:16

LONG, LONG AGO, IN THE MEDIEVAL VILLAGE OF CRACOW in what is now Poland, there lived a poor and pious old rabbi named Eisik, son of Jekel. One night Eisik was called by a dream. The dream told him to make the journey to Prague, many days' arduous travel away. There, beneath the great sprawl of the bridge that led to the royal castle, he would find a treasure trove of gold that would change his life.

At first, he shrugged it off, pretending that he didn't believe in dreams. But when he had the same dream the next night, and then a third time, Eisik decided that he had better heed the call and make the journey.

Several nights later, he arrived in Prague and discovered the bridge but was dismayed to see it guarded by soldiers. The rabbi felt thwarted that he couldn't immediately dig for his fortune under the bridge, so he lingered helplessly. A plangent rain began to fall. Up and down the riverbank he prowled, until he was stopped by the captain of the guard, who asked if he had lost something. The rabbi said no, but that he had come a long way to find something. Then he revealed his dream about the hidden cache of gold underneath the bridge.

"Gold!" the captain blurted out. He couldn't keep himself from laughing, then admonished the rabbi for believing in dreams. "What reasonable man takes them seriously?" he asked. "As a matter of fact, I heard a voice call out in an absurd dream just a few nights ago, urging me to take the long journey to Cracow and visit a rabbi, Eisik, son of Jekel. The voice told me look in the recess behind his stove where I would find a gold treasure."

Shaking his head in disbelief, the captain warned the rabbi about

Wooden boats floating on the Vltava River, near the Charles Bridge, Prague, Czech Republic.

the sin of gullibility and went back to his post. Rabbi Eisik hurried home and, once inside, searched behind his stove, and there found the treasure that ended his poverty and did indeed change his life.

This tale, rediscovered by Martin Buber in his *Tales of the Hasidim*, illuminates one of the supreme paradoxes: If the treasure—the truth of our life—is so close at hand, why is it so difficult for us to wake up, rub our eyes, and reach out to find what is within arm's reach? Why waste time and money and risk our necks to venture somewhere far, far away? The great scholar of Hinduism Heinrich Zimmer saw in the story a parable that embraces one of the central dilemmas of human existence.

"And so, the real treasure," Zimmer reflects, "the treasure that brings our wretchedness and our ordeals to an end, is never far away. We must never go looking for it in distant lands, for it lies buried in the most secret recesses of our own house; in other words, of our own being. It is behind the stove, the life- and heat-giving center that governs our existence, the heart of our hearth, if only we know how to dig for it. But then there is the strange and constant fact that it is only after a pious journey to a distant region, in a strange land, a new country, that the meaning of the inner voice guiding our search can be revealed to us. And added to that strange and constant fact there is another: that the person who reveals the meaning of our mysterious inner voyage to us must himself be a stranger, of another faith and another race."

"The strange and constant fact" that Zimmer refers to is at the core of the mysterious drawing power of pilgrimage. All of the answers are within us, but such is our tendency toward forgetting that we sometimes need to venture to a faraway land to tap our own memory. Our intuitive self has shut down; our light into the transcendent has gone out.

"The archaic image of the soul is likened to treasure hidden in the midst of the body," wrote the distinguished professor of religion Mircea Eliade.

The irrepressible desire to see deeply into ourselves and the world evokes what Hindus call *dyana*, "the long pure look." The desire is also at the heart of our attraction to ancient ruins. Seeing the tumble-down stones of the Colosseum in Rome, the earthworks of Babylon,

the ramparts of Troy, or
the undulations of the
Serpent Mound in Ohio
is for many travelers like
looking into images of
the soul of a culture or
era worn down by time.
A charged imagination
fills in the missing
columns, restores the
rooftops of buildings,
projects the past glory of
entire cities and civilizations.

There are many
ways that individuals
and cultures can, and
do, lose their souls. To
our peril, we forget that
the gold is at hand; we
forget that there is a hidden door, a secret room
in all our lives. The
force behind myths,
fairytales, parables, and
soulful travel stories
reveals the myriad ways

Opera singer Cathy Devor, of Vermont, tests the world-renowned acoustics of the Great Theater at Ephesus, Turkey, where Herodotus wrote, St. Paul preached, the Virgin Mary died, and the Temple of Artemis amazed the ancient world.

the sacred breaks through the resistance and shines forth into our
world. Pilgrimage holds out the promise of personal contact with that
sacred force.

Many pilgrimages begin with the calling of a dream, like Rabbi
Eisik's. Some come by night, others by day. Rather than accompany

their friends on an around-the-world cruise, an elderly couple I know, Bob and June, decided to spend their life savings on what they called their dream trip—a journey to Jerusalem to walk the *Via Dolorosa,* to follow in the footsteps of Christ. "We have been frivolous," they told their children. "Now is the time for us to renew our faith." In his book *American Places,* William Zinsser tells how he felt called to rediscover America. One of the most touching stories he heard on his pilgrimage was told by a guide at Mark Twain's house in Hannibal, Missouri. She related that when the blind Argentinian writer Jorge Luis Borges visited the States, he fulfilled a lifelong dream to visit Twain's hometown. He asked to be led down to the shores of the Big Muddy—the Mississippi. Then he bent down and touched the waters of the surging river and said, "Now my pilgrimage is complete."

There is another call, the one that arrives the day when what once worked no longer does. Sometimes people need a shock; sometimes a tocsin call. It is time for a wake-up call. A man is fired from a job; a child runs away from home; ulcers overtake the body. The ancients called this "soul loss." Today, the equivalent is the loss of meaning or purpose in our lives. There is a void where there should be what Gerard Manley Hopkins calls "juice and joy." The heart grows cold; life loses its vitality. Our accomplishments seem meaningless.

As Tolstoy wrote in his *Confessions,* "Nothing ahead except ruins." We seem to be in the thick of the forest without a road. "What, then, must we do?"

The long line of myths, legends, poetry, and stories throughout the world tell us that it is at that moment of darkness that the call comes. It arrives in various forms—an itch, a fever, an offer, a ringing, an inspiration, an idea, a voice, words in a book that seem to have been written just for us—or a knock.

THE KNOCK

The truth knocks on the door and you say, "Go away.
I'm looking for the truth," and so it goes away. Puzzling.
—Robert Pirsig

In his magnificent work *The Great Travelers*, Milton Rugoff writes that "a bewildering variety of motives drives our traveler."

"When a moment knocks on the door of your life," wrote Russian novelist Boris Pasternak, "it is often no louder than the beating of your heart, and it is very easy to miss it." In Matthew 7:7, we find: "Ask, and it shall be given you; Seek and ye shall find; Knock, and it shall be opened unto you."

The moment of the knock, the *strong time*, the ripe time, was personified by the Greeks as the god Kairos. They envisioned him with winged feet and scepter, poised on a razor's edge, left hand inches away from the scales of Fate. The god also symbolized chance, fortune, and synchronicity, which is another kind of knocking at the door. The invocation for the god was "Grab Him Swiftly." Chances are, the myth says, the moment is sweeping past. Fortune may not soon pass this way again, and this moment of time—never again.

For sculptor Max Ernst, the call was heard from within the stone for him to scratch "the runes of our own mystery." Poet Gary Snyder remarks that the moment of inspiration is so fleeting that he has to be ready, which is why he always carries a cheap spiral notebook and pen with him. What drove Marlowe and imprinted destiny into his soul in Joseph Conrad's *Heart of Darkness* was a vision from childhood:

I would look for hours at South America, or Africa, or Australia, and lose myself in all the glories of exploration. At that time there were many blank spaces on the earth, and when I saw one that looked particularly inviting on a map (but they all look like

*that) I would put my finger on it and say, When I grow up I
will go there.*

For the twelfth-century Islamic mystic Mevlana Rumi, the source is
as close as the vein in your neck. "I have lived on the lip of insanity,
wanting to know reasons, knocking on a door. It opens. I've been
knocking from the inside."

While traveling in Thailand, I was struck by the beauty of the bells
rung each morning, and throughout the day, from the village monasteries. Each time the bells were sounded, the monks and practicing
Buddhists would pause for a moment in whatever they were doing—
riding a bicycle, hoeing a rice paddy—and bring full attention to their breath, their state of mind, at that precise moment, and then move on, restored. In a small town in Cappadocia, Turkey, I came to appreci-ate the raucous cry of the muezzin from the crackling speakers of the minaret. Five times a day, the call to prayer went out across the valley, bringing men and women to the mosque. In its wake came a stillness that seemed to revive the town for hours afterward. In Thomas Moore's *Medi-tations*, he gives a loving description of the centering

*A young Buddhist monk raps a bronze bell
in the tower of his monastery in the village of
Sukhothai, Thailand.*

power of the angelus bells each day when he lived in a monastery.

To hear the pounding on the door, we have to remember to pay attention to what we have lost and to what is calling for us. Not a day goes by when the world doesn't cry out for us, signal us with signs and sounds, calling us home. Listening closely is nearly a lost art, but a retrievable one. The soul thrives on it.

Words heard by chance have been known to change lives.

Imagine, as poet Antonio Machado did, how "the wind, one brilliant day, called." Think of the ways you have been called in the past, toward the love of your life. How did you find the work you are doing now? The city where you live? Your soulmate? How much of this was intentional? Sheer dint of will? How much was by chance, hunch, accident, or good fortune?

The call to the sacred journey your secret heart longs for won't come by expectation, will not arrive in a logical way. If you imagine that something is trying to call to you, try to practice stillness for a few minutes each day. Be still and quiet and you may be surprised what you start to hear. The other component of becoming open to such a call is the practice of solitude. Remember Rilke's words to the young poet: "The necessary thing is after all but this: solitude, great inner solitude. . . . What goes on in your innermost being is worthy of your whole love; you must somehow keep working at it and not lose too much time and too much courage in clarifying your attitude toward people."

Ask yourself what is *absurd* in your life right now. Then recall that the roots of the word refer to being "deaf." If you have stopped listening, try to begin again, first with what you love, then with what is difficult for you.

Something may be trying to reach you—a voice, a destiny.

THE CALLING FORTH

*Most people have that fantasy of catching
the train that whistles in the night.*
—Willie Nelson

From 1970 to 1974, I studied at the University of Detroit during the day and worked in a steel factory at night. I had a scholarship for college but needed to support my family, which had just been split apart like cordwood by divorce. The first year was just manageable, twenty to twenty-five hours a week. But by my senior year, I was working midnight shifts, accumulating more than sixty hours a week.

All year I flailed against my fate. I was offered my dream job by my writing idol, Joe Falls at the *Detroit Free Press*, as a cub reporter in the sports department.

Despite the glamorous vision of that future, I knew that going straight from classes and the factory into a career would make me seethe with rage and resentment.

With six months to go before graduation, my foreman, an ex-Green Beret named Bob Schnekenburger, began coaxing me to keep going, to not give up my dream of writing, but also not to stay around Detroit. He urged me to get out while I still could and see the world. During every break, while the giant and thunderous presses stamped out steel nuts for the cars that rolled out of Motor City, he shouted stories at me about the rock gardens of Kyoto, the bars of Singapore, the rice paddies of the Philippines, the cafés of Paris.

Over the course of that last year in Detroit, early in the morning before punching my time card, feeling no more human than the behemoths around me, I took a black marker and wrote on the back of my locker in large swirling letters the names of all the places I planned to visit after graduation, after my life in the factories:

Paris, Prague, Dublin, Moscow, Rome, Copenhagen, the Rhine

River, Munich, Oktoberfest, Cairo, Karnak, Saigon, Belgium,
London, Stonehenge, Pamplona, Rio de Janeiro, the Arctic Circle,
the Seven Seas, Budapest, Warsaw, Edinburgh, Jerusalem,
Athens, Bangkok, Singapore, Madrid, Tokyo

Mine was an unabashedly young and romantic vision, which drew sarcastic comments from most of my fellow factory rats. Yet every time I opened that creaky, oil-stained locker door, I felt the call of the outside world, to the future, and away from my land of death. The practice of luring the world toward me, calling forth my own adventures, has stayed with me ever since. I've played rhapsodies on that theme over and over, believing implicitly in the power of names to entrance us. I've learned since that to name something is to imbue it with soul.

For the young French boy René Caillié, the lure was a single word: Timbuktu. He heard it one day as a boy in a village in Burgundy, and his destiny was immediately imprinted in his soul. From that moment on, Caillié's single ambition in life was to be the first Westerner to catch sight of the legendary forbidden city in the north African desert. Twenty years later, in 1865, after studying the desert languages, committing the Koran to heart, and learning the gestures of Arab traders and Bedouins, Caillié walked unnoticed into Timbuktu.

To the young Frenchwoman Isabelle Eberhardt, the call came from her readings of travelers moving anonymously through northern Africa; they inspired her to set out and live the rest of her days far away from the manacles of traditional European society. For contemporary writer Viviane Wayne, the call came from a hundred-year-old faded photograph of her mother as a young girl dressed for a Turkish bath. Wayne was handed the photo from a distant cousin while on a brief stopover in Istanbul, and the startling image prompted her story "A Sensual Pilgrimage to a Turkish Bath."

Always, the call summons us to the hidden life.

THE SACRED CALL

Personal answers to ultimate questions.
That is what we seek.
—Alexander Eliot

A ll ancient pilgrimage not only celebrated identity," write Simon Colman and John Elsner in their book *Pilgrimage*, "but did so by linking it with a special place." The Great Panathenaea was an ancient procession that wove together the sacred and the secular as it wound up the Acropolis to the Parthenon, where a new robe was offered to the gold-and-ivory statue of Athena. If a spectator arrived at any other time, their circumambulation of the temple, according to the authors, "constituted a kind of proxy pilgrimage, a vicarious pilgrimage in a sacred event scheduled for a different time."

The Olympic Games were inaugurated in 776 B.C.E. in Olympia, Greece, in honor of the god Zeus. Thousands from all over the Mediterranean ventured there or to other events and sites such as the Pythian Games, the Isthmian Games, the Nemean, and Delphi, and were guaranteed safe passage by an unusual suspension of war during the games. Other sacred-center pilgrimages included Phocia, Dodona, and Ammon in Libya.

Steve Shrope, an engineer and artist from Detroit, Michigan, fulfilled a lifelong dream by making a pilgrimage to Greece to see its architectural splendors, most notably the Parthenon, in Athens.

Men and women alike came to these places, compelled by a call for supernatural healing, oracular solutions, or the need to exhibit solidarity with their fellow citizens in their home city.

Among Australian aborigines, there is a phenomenon known as "walkabout." The call for the long walk into the outback to visit ancestral grounds can come at a moment's notice. On the scaffolding of high-rise projects in Sydney, at a gas station in Darwin, or in poor shack housing, men and women are known to rise up, drop their lunch buckets, paychecks, and children, and begin to walk. As if in a trance, they walk the holy ground of "invisible pathways which meander all over Australia," as Bruce Chatwin describes them, "and are known to Europeans as 'Dreaming Tracks' or 'Songlines'; to the Aboriginals as the 'Footprints of the Ancestors' or the 'Way of the Law.'"

Chatwin, one of the greatest chroniclers of the nomadic urge, writes:

I have a vision of the Songlines stretching across the continents and the ages; that wherever men have trodden they have left a trail of song (of which we may, now and then, catch an echo); and that these trails must reach back, in time and space, to an isolated pocket in the African savannah, where the First Man opening his mouth in defiance of the terrors that surrounded him, shouted the opening stanza of the World Song "I AM!"

For members of the Comanche Nation, the call for a vision quest comes during adolescence. Vincent Parker, great-grandson of the great chief Quanah Parker, told me in 1988 about the moment of his great-grandfather's awakening: "He went out to the Staked Plains not for himself but for his people. He heard the call of the eagle and he went, just like that. He didn't ask any questions. He knew his people needed healing, so he went. And he sat out there for four days and for four nights. In the middle of the fourth night the vision of White Buffalo came to him and told him that his Indian nation would need a little extra, something to help them through the death times to come. And that's when Quanah knew he had to ride during the next Comanche Moon [October] down there to Mexico and get himself some of that peyote, so his people could have their visions, even after they lost their land, their religion, their language."

THE CALL FROM THE HILL

When it is unbearably difficult, go to the Hill of Crosses.
—Dalia Striagate, Lithuanian writer

In the fall of 1996, my Lithuanian friend Sarunas Marciulionis, the first European to play in the NBA and three-time Olympic medal winner, invited me to visit him in his homeland. I was deeply moved by his desire to "share the soul of my country with you." I liked the sound of that. The offer came at a time when I was losing faith in the world of books and films and even friendship.

Late one night, in the bar of Sarunas' hotel in Vilnius, we discussed what he called the "soul food" of his country—music, poetry, and their national basketball team. "But if you really want to know my country," he said in between shots of vodka, "you must see the Hill of Crosses. That is where you will find it revealed—the soul of the Lithuanian people. In 1991, a man carried a 200-pound cross on his back across Europe just to place it there. He said he heard a voice that he had to do something to keep Lithuanian culture alive."

That night I read up on the curious history of the site, and early the next morning I was driven three hours from Vilnius through long tracts of the last untouched pine forests in Europe, past medieval villages where haywagons are still pulled by donkeys. We were en route to one of the strangest of all sacred sites in the world: *Kryziu Kalnas*,

A forest of crosses are silhouetted against the late afternoon sky at the Hill of Crosses, Siauliai, Lithuania, a place of national pilgrimage.

While reciting a prayer, a pilgrim makes her offering of a handmade crucifix to the holy ground that has come to symbolize freedom itself to the people of Lithuania.

the Forest of Crosses, the Hill of Prayers, the Lithuanian Golgotha. The Hill of Crosses.

When we arrived at the site, the makeshift parking lot had a few cars, a school bus, and a few dilapidated tour buses, from which dozens of pilgrims shuffled out and made their way toward the hundred-foot-high hill. Hundreds of thousands of crosses are spiked into the holy ground. I read that this hill is one of more than 600 anomalous mounds in the relentlessly flat landscape. The old Livonian chronicles suggest that a castle was built here centuries ago. But the legend and the source of the hill's power dates back only to 1850, as the site of a victorious battle against the Swedes. Ever since, patriots and true believers have been making long pilgrimages to plant crosses of every size, substance, and description into its sacred ground.

The day was overcast, even gloomy. I stood in the light mist with Sarunas' friend. He made a furtive sign of the cross as we approached the hill, which is a beehive of crosses, a tangled forest of crucifixes, an ant heap of folk art. Made of wood, iron, plastic, and brass, the crosses glint in the rain; they tinkle in the wind. Some are painstakingly carved—true works of art depicting Christ in agony; others are slap-dash creations tossed on the pile as a quick gesture of devotion. Crosses are stacked, hurled, draped, clustered, grouped; bare or adorned with photographs, paintings, statues of the Virgin Mary, or the crucified Christ. The crosses hold images of family members deported to Siberia on trumped-up charges; some mourn with the weight of photographs of Lithuanians who died during the Nazi occupation. They have been carried on the shoulders of pilgrims from all corners of Lithuania, those who heard a wailing deep in their soul to make their mark, leave a votive offering, to beseech God for a favor or thank Him for recent blessings. But mostly, the crosses serve to boldly declare the Lithuanians' irrepressible desire for freedom.

At the top of the hill, I read a startling description from a local writer: "We twin our sad eyes to the crosses. Suffering is the inevitable part of the earthly existence. It adds the real meaning to our lives. Put up a cross when you suffer."

From 1917 to 1985 the Soviets bulldozed the hill again and again out of disdain for the "ignorance and fanaticism" that it represented to them. But the bulldozers and threats of deportation could not prevent the "pilgrims, patriots, and pietists" from returning at night to start over. Especially those with the life-sized, self-carved crosses carried along the Via Dolorosas of Lithuania in constant displays of spiritual resistance to the occupation. As one recent pilgrim put it, the site is "a very vivid relic of our past [that] rests on a tiny hill and reminds us of our cruel and glorious history—uprisings, wars, revolutions, occupations...."

From the top of the hill, I saw dozens of peasants who had walked, ridden bicycles, or come in buses to pray at the holy site. The site sprawled over local fields surrounding the mound, one end of it uncoiling like the tail of a serpent just roused from a long slumber. The strange charm of pilgrimage sites all over the world is compacted on this small hill: Its chaos is its charm, its kitsch, its soul.

Finally, the gadflies won. Gorbachev finally gave up the long Soviet bulldozer campaign in 1985, announcing quietly, "Let them have their hill." Two years later, emboldened students in Vilnius began to demonstrate for Lithuanian independence. The call was heard all over the world.

Back in Vilnius later that night, Sarunas summed up the symbolic power of the hill: "Just knowing that it was there made the fight for independence much easier."

THE CALL OF DESTINY

The longest journey
Is the journey inwards
Of him who has chosen his destiny
—Dag Hammarskjöld

In the 1970s, a young American lawyer named Eric Lawton was backpacking around the world. In his third year on the road, he arrived in Paris, faced with a difficult decision. Within days, he was scheduled to return to Los Angeles and his law practice, a notion that engendered mixed feelings after his many adventures. Lost in thought, he found himself wandering around the Latin Quarter and finally over the Pont des Artes and into the mighty fortress of world art—the Louvre. For hours, he drifted through the busy galleries, the master-works obscured by the turbulent crowd.

Finally, he found himself—and I think he would agree with the phrase—standing in front of a painting by Rembrandt, *The Philosopher*, an image of an ancient man deep in thought, seated by the window, a winding stair descending from the stone walls, an old woman tending the hearth fire. Three hours later, he was still there, lost in the chia-roscuro, the magical mixture of golden light, shadow, and mystery that is the confluence of the Dutch master's genius. In a way that mystifies Lawton to this day, he heard a voice that afternoon which changed his life. The voice told him that he must follow another call, the one toward art. For him that meant one thing: photography.

When Eric returned home, he gathered together three years of photographs from his travels and made of them a new life. He made a vow to continue his pilgrimages to the most sacred places on the planet and to express in imagery what he found there.

In contrast, the shadowcatcher Ansel Adams, who believed that his camera was a combination of machine and spirit, wrote in his autobi-ography about one afternoon that shaped his destiny. He was married and in his twenties and still living with his mother and aunt. The time had come when he had to choose between his two great passions—photography and piano. His wife, Virginia, told him she would support him in whatever he believed to be his true calling, but his mother pleaded in anguish, "Do not give up the piano! The camera cannot express the human soul!"

Adams paused for a moment, then replied with the confidence of the moment, "Perhaps the camera cannot, but the photographer can."

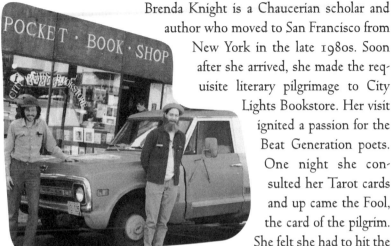

Brenda Knight is a Chaucerian scholar and author who moved to San Francisco from New York in the late 1980s. Soon after she arrived, she made the requisite literary pilgrimage to City Lights Bookstore. Her visit ignited a passion for the Beat Generation poets. One night she consulted her Tarot cards and up came the Fool, the card of the pilgrim. She felt she had to hit the road, follow the thread of this fascination back to New York. "I felt called to make the pilgrimage back to the source of the creek,"

Poets Jeff Poniewaz and Antler make a ritual visit to City Lights Bookstore, San Francisco, before returning to their home in Milwaukee, Wisconsin, 1986.

as she puts it, "the place where it all began for the Beats. How else are you going to know about them unless you go?"

In New York, she made her way to Allen Ginsberg's haunts, the Cedar Tavern, all the places that Pollock, Corso, Jannine Pommie Vega, and Kerouac had hung out. "At Ginsberg's apartment, I looked at his door and on the molding there was a big scrape mark, as if from a break-in attempt by some desperate creature. There was an air of desperation, but I felt like I had made a mysterious connection with them. I kept up my research, especially into Kerouac. He was truly the one. I believed there was some kind of fate that drew us together. Walking in his footsteps through Greenwich Village was like going to the Holy of Holies—you don't need to go to church if you can go to the source of great literature."

I asked how her pilgrimage had influenced her authorship of the groundbreaking book *Women of the Beat Generation*. She replied, "When things have gotten tough, I've figured, if Kerouac did it, I can do it. What better way to understand the secret of a writer's creativity than to walk in their path?"

For scholar of Mayan culture and archaeology tour leader Michael Guillén, the call came when he was a boy, but he didn't know he had followed it until years later. "When I was a boy, I used to break off branches," he recollects. "I used to create little wooden men with the sticks. Recently, when I was making a pilgrimage in the mountains of Guatemala, to the Maya god Maximon, a syncretic Guatemalan highland deity made out of branches. I suddenly realized that this was a mirror image of my childhood creations! This is why I like childhood memories; they help tell us who we are or who we will become if we

A Mayan woman from the highlands of Guatemala spends an afternoon contemplating the snail-shaped El Caracol, the ancient Mayan astronomical observatory at Chichen Itza, Yucatan, Mexico.

are unfolding spiritually. Another revelation came to me recently when a travel companion told me on our journey through Mexico that he always knew where I'd been because I left spirals behind in the dirt paths to the temples. He was right. I looked at them and realized that they were counterclockwise ones, which I learned later are maps of the effort toward the spirit."

Joan Marler is a dancer and mythologist. She considers the call to embark on a sacred journey as part of the longing she feels not only in her mind, but in her body. This restlessness has impelled her on spiritual quests all over the world, to Ireland, Malta, Lithuania, and Russia, where she feels the ancient energies of the world come alive, which, in turn, makes her feel more alive.

"For many women, going on a sacred journey means getting back in touch with what is sacred in the earth. That's what I feel has come up in our time. First there is the personal restlessness, the feeling of being nowhere in the place they are now; then there is the need to feel something deeper than the surface glare of things, a longing to be somewhere else where that is possible.

"For me it's as if the 'story comes by' in the form of pictures in a book, fragments of poetry, or stories (especially myths) that somehow constellate the longing in me. A voice says, "Oh, perhaps over there is the potential for my fruition."

In 1990, Jo Beaton was in a job that was consuming her creative spirit. She began to dream of images from the myths she was reading about for her work at a publishing house and decided to take action. She contacted her mother and aunt and convinced them to take a journey with her to the Mediterranean, and even sent them books about the goddess sites there to help them prepare along with her.

"Dreaming about the possibilities is heart-swelling stuff," she recalls. "It was empowering to learn that there once was a time in which the world was calm, a time when great goddesses were worshipped, and societies were matrilineal, war-shunning, nature-loving, guided by both women and men in peaceful partnership. Such studying and dreaming led me to embark on a very personal pilgrimage to the ruins of some of these ancient civilizations. To believe that 6,000 years ago, lasting for thousands of years, there was a viable, nonpatriarchal world, with its own complicated and vibrant myths, symbols, and rituals, gave me the very personal hope that I could glean something from the legacy of what the eminent archaeologist Marija Gimbutas called 'Old Europe' and apply it to my existence here, now in late-twentieth-century 'modern' life. The trio of my mother, my aunt, and me ventured forth by plane and train, boat and bus—first to Crete, to the Minoan goddess site at the labyrinthine palace of Knossos on that remote Greek island, seeking truths, visions, and some inspiration to carry on."

Imagine the last time your faith failed. Faith in yourself, your family, your God, your country, love, the arts, even faith itself. Of course, faith is Janus-faced. One face is blind, unquestioning; the other sees far and deep, trusting what is unfolding in you, in life. It takes courage to trust the voices that may or may not be genuine calls. With that in mind, what or where has called to you recently? A Lourdes of the soul? A Graceland of the heart? Are you curious to see where Jane Austen lived or where Dante first saw Beatrice?

Think about the notion that there is a "cure" in the practice of curiosity, as author Greg Levoy uncovers in his book *Callings*. Maybe curiosity didn't kill the cat; maybe it *thrilled* the cat, and contemplation brought her back. Where does your curiosity lead you now? Have you seen a movie like *Zorba the Greek* that makes you hunger to dance on a beach on Crete, or read a book such as Laurens van der Post's *Venture to the Interior* that haunts you with images about Africa for months afterward? What "submerged recollections" in van der Post's wonderful phrase, rising now and then like islands in the Pacific, reveal the hidden source of your brooding?

The range of journeys that hearken to these calls confirms for me how strange is the workshop of fate. At an indoor café in Budapest several years ago, a Hungarian woman leaned across the table from me and inquired if I was American. I nodded. She whispered that she had just returned from California and, after a melancholic pause, confessed that her favorite spot was the steps of Sproul Hall at UC Berkeley, where Mario Savio had ignited the free-speech movement in the 1960s.

"I am a reporter here in eastern Europe," she explained, steeling her voice. "When I got a chance to go to America, I said no to your Disneylands and your Studio Universals, and left my travel group because I had to see the place where people stopped a war."

The sacred pours forth through openings we never imagined possible, until we hear about them in the voices of people who have made great journeys to witness it.

When I hear these stories from strangers all around the world, I think about Emerson and his love of stories and conversation, and how he once said that he would walk a hundred miles through a snowstorm to have one good conversation. Now there's a man who heard the call and returned it.

"Our lives are woven from a melody of calls that draw us out and help us to define ourselves," writes David Spangler in his book *The Call.*

Can you see your tapestry emerging, hear your song?

If the world truly is "wild at heart and weird on top," as Barry Gifford would have us believe, surely there will be pilgrimages there.

Case in point: In 1990, Romanian-born poet, social satirist, and National Public Radio commentator Andrei Codrescu took a call from a TV producer. The man invited him to make a movie about the weird roadside attractions in Florida. Codrescu was interested, but had a problem: He couldn't drive. They asked if he'd like to learn.

"Would I like to drive?" he asks rhetorically in his insanely funny book *Road Scholar*. "Would a fish like to fly? Would a child like to grow up? Would an elephant like to be a swan? Was it a matter of *wanting to*, or was it more like an impossible cross-species dream, a magical transformation?"

Eventually, Codrescu learned to drive, firing the pistons on the engine of a hilarious documentary film about his trip across America in a candy-apple-red '68 Cadillac convertible. But, believing that foreigners are in search of a fantasy America that never existed, he set off in quest of the *strangest* aspects of his adopted country. Though he foresaw that there was "something vast and scary too in the jillions of driving-and-heartbreak songs" throbbing on the car radio in the miles ahead, he also saw an opportunity.

"Here was a chance for me to transform myself once more, to begin again," he writes. "I love being born again, and I practice it. It's my passion, also my *métier*, my specialty. Changing names, places of residence, body shapes, opinions ... what endless delight. America was set up for this kind of thing, a vast stage for projecting images of self that Europe had made impossible."

For Codrescu, the road ahead suggested Al Capone, Henry Miller, Jack Kerouac, and Huck Finn, the panoply of renegade pilgrims in American folklore. Skeptical that "the road" even exists anymore, and feeling at times like "an encyclopedia of dangerous knowledge" he set out to fulfill his own lifelong dream.

THE TOWER

The world is a traveler's inn
—Afghan folk saying

I am "circling and circling" around an ancient idea, like Rilke around the ancient tower, wondering if he is "a falcon, a storm, or a great song." I am circumambulating like William Butler Yeats around his tower outside Galway, wondering if the center is going to hold. I am gazing at Michel de Montaigne's tower in the land my family comes from in the south of France, wondering about the mad genius of mental peregrinations.

What is the urge, the impulse, the notion, the idea that leads to the call for us to move at all costs to the central axis of each of our different worlds, the cosmic center, the source of all we believe in? This is a question that has haunted me since boyhood, when I saw the notices on the church bulletin board for trips to Lourdes, Fatima, Guadalupe. I was doubly intrigued to hear stories from the nuns at school about the penance that

The journey of the pilgrim toward God is symbolized in the upward spiraling ramp of the ninth-century Minaret of the Mosque, Samarra, Iraq.

could be worked off by completing a sanctioned pilgrimage, and the spiritual merit you could earn. In my young imagination, I pictured the soul as a chalkboard on which God added and subtracted points throughout the miserable sinner's life. But pilgrimage, I was told early on, had the miraculous effect of erasing sins. Through sacrifice and prayer, a person could gain forgiveness. Later, I would learn about the belief in "merit" earned on pilgrimage in Buddhist and Hindu traditions, as well as the notion of transformation implicit in secular pilgrimages, such as the writer's journey to Paris or the artist's to Rome.

I am proposing a way of looking not only *at* but *through* the road, through our moments of travel to their past and future dimensions, to consider each encounter as a chapter in a long novel, each person along the way as one of the characters in our soul journey through life.

What I am seeking are "equivalents," as photographer Alfred Stieglitz called his photographs, which evoked something strangely similar deep in the viewer. I am assembling a "correspondence of things," like Pythagoras, who regarded the way the things of the world mirror each other.

These are ways to learn to live in the "marvelous moment," in the words of Vietnamese monk Thich Nhat Hanh, and listen to the "calls from the Buddha." What is more miraculous than the moment? he asks. Being human and fallible, he gently reminds us, our minds are prone to wandering, and if they do, we may miss out on our true calling.

Imagine slowing down, becoming aware of the voices in your dreams, your unexpected encounters. The decision to take a journey always redoubles my respect for time. I literally end up "looking again" at the role it plays in my life. Often, I have thought about those awe-inspired medieval pilgrims to the Temple of Time in Rome, where the first public clock was displayed. Crowds waited for hours to file past the

elaborate clockworks, torn between admiration for the wondrous preci-
sion, and suspicion, for they knew that *their* time was no longer theirs.

Recalling can help clarify the calls to come. Practice listening—to
your friends, your children, music, the wind, your dreams, the ancient
wisdom of sacred texts. Listen as though your life depended on it.

It does.

THE PILGRIM'S TASKS

We must find our touchstones
where we can.
—John Berryman

For centuries, a mysterious
flintlike stone called the
"touchstone" has been used to
test the purity of gold. Rubbing or
pressing the waxlike ball over the
stone leaves streaks behind that
can tell the discriminating eye the
true value of the gold. Hence, anything that helps us see whether
something, even a place or destination, is the real thing, authentic, if it is "gold," can be a
touchstone. The touchstone is a
brilliant metaphor for an attitude
or state of mind that can test the
sacred dimension.

Once you have committed to
your journey, it's time to bring out
the touchstone. It's time to listen

This statue of French philosopher
Michel de Montaigne, across from the
Sorbonne in Paris, has inspired the
custom among students of touching his
boot before exams, perhaps in the hope
that the innovator of the "essay" might
inspire their own efforts.

to the pilgrim mood in you, to the one who wants to explore the heart and soul of the land you are about to visit. It's time to decide when to leave on your journey, during what season and what break in your own life, time to determine if you should depart alone or with a group. Time to take time seriously.

One of the methods I've used through the years to "call" my journey closer to me as my preparations are underway is to find myths, short stories, poetry, the sacred writing of the land I am about to visit. It helps me begin the inner adjustment, the creating of a new world to explore. For my travels through Turkey, I read two books of Sufi poetry, one by Rumi, the other an anthology of the great Sufi mystics. Each morning before I left, I read a page of poetry and teaching stories; by the time I landed in Turkey, my soul was already there waiting for me. Every day of my journey, from The Mystic Tea and Smoking Garden in Istanbul to Rumi's tomb in Konya, I continued to read the great mystic's work, and each time felt his ancient presence. Timeless art is like that. It anticipates you. Without it there is no sacred journey.

One of my fondest travel "calls" was the moment I opened a large envelope with a postmark from Ottawa, Canada. I was mystified, not remembering any relatives from there. Inside was a six-page mimeographed program for the 1995 Monette Family Reunion, to be held at Lake Nipissing, Ontario. Still confused, I read on only to discover that Cyril and Odile Monette were my great-great-grandparents on my grandmother Olive's side. A startling black-and-white photograph of them graced the front page of the announcement, a kind of Canadian Gothic image of two stern, backwoods ancestors poised in front of a log cabin.

To prepare for the adventure, I found a book called *Les Voyageurs*, a history of the trappers in the French Canadian wilderness that my great-grandfather Charlemagne had been part of. Shortly afterward, I found a tape of the "paddling songs" that the *voyageurs* sang on their long canoe trips. By playing it for months before our trip, I coaxed the pilgrim soul out of me.

Two latter-day voyageur canoes rest on a glacier rock in Lake Nipissing, Ontario, Canada.

Six months later, my partner Jo and I were canoeing down the French River with seventeen of my cousins, reenacting the original voyage of my ancestor settlers. When we arrived in Monetville, fifty miles and three days later, there were 1,500 relatives huddled in the dawn fog. In the few minutes it took us to come ashore, it was as if a hundred years of family history unspooled on an enormous movie projector. Returning to the lake my father took me to as a boy, coming back to the source of my family history, as with all pilgrimages, brought home for me, in every sense of the word, that I was part of a continuum.

Imagine playing the Surrealist's game called *Le Voyage Magique*, in which the players choose a journey to places picked at random. Pilgrimage is an imaginary road with real stones in it. You can twist an ankle—or find a way to glide past the obstacles—just dreaming about it. Spin a globe, riffle the pages of an atlas, play pin the flag on the map. Do you trust in fate? Are you tantalized by the dream that somewhere, as novelist James Salter has mused, the *true* life is being led, that there are venerable things to learn down the road?

When you commit to that dream, invisible hands will appear to guide you. Mythologist Joseph Campbell knew this from his circumnavigation of world myths, as well as from his own life experience. He was able to say with conviction that when you hearken to the call to adventure, "when you follow your bliss, doors will open where there were no doors before." By *bliss* he meant the deepest fascination of your life. Follow that impulse, to Glastonbury, Canterbury, Borobudur, or your ancestral homeland, and all manner of favors will come your way.

As the philosopher Goethe insisted,

> *Whatever you can do, or dream you can, begin it.*
> *Boldness has genius, power and magic in it.*

III

DEPARTURE

Give me my Scallop shell of quiet,
My staffe of Faith to walke upon,
My Scrip of Joy, Immortall diet,
My bottle of salvation:
My Gowne of Glory, hopes true gage,
And thus Ile take my pilgrimage.

—Sir Walter Raleigh,
The Pilgrimage (1604)

"THERE ARE FOUR ROADS," BEGINS THE TWELFTH-CENTURY GUIDEBOOK *The Pilgrim's Guide*, "which, leading to Santiago, converge to form a single road at Puente la Reina in Spanish territory. One crosses Saint-Gilles, Montpellier, Toulouse, and the pass of Somport; another goes through Nôtre Dame of Le Puy, Sainte-Foy of Conques, and Saint Pierre of Moissac; another traverses Sainte-Marie-Madeleine of Vézelay, Saint-Léonard in the Limousin, as well as the city of Périgueux; still another cuts through Saint-Jean-d'Angély, Sainte-Eutrope of Saintes, and the city of Bordeaux. . . ."

The purpose of this incantatory listing of place-names was to inspire the medieval pilgrims departing on their sacred but dangerous journeys and to give a measure of comfort that there was a world beyond theirs that could be mapped and measured.

I've been fascinated with the Santiago pilgrimage ever since I became intrigued with the scallop shells I saw embedded in houses around Paris when I lived there in the late 1980s. Other than French aesthetics, I wondered why someone would display a shell on the lintel of their doorway or their windowsill. Over time, I've come to appreciate the motivation, realizing that my habit of displaying photographs and creating altars of travel souvenirs is scarcely different from the response of medieval travelers. The scallop shells were the proud symbols of returned pilgrims from the legendary shrine of Saint James the Apostle at Santiago de Compostela, in Galicia on Spain's northwest Atlantic coast.

For medieval pilgrims, the journey had many meanings. The times were steeped in mysticism, rife with cultist devotion. Many of those

departed with the hopes that coming into contact with the saint's venerated relics would heal them; after all, Saint James was considered the
thaumaturge, the miracle-maker. Others longed for self-purification,
believing in the catharsis of an arduous journey and the merits of constant prayer. These sojourners met other kinds of pilgrims en route,
including widely ostracized "false pilgrims" hired by others to make
the journey for them, or criminals whose sentence was the penance of
completing the pilgrimage. Common to all pilgrims was the sense of
awakened wonder. The long and wearying way carried them through
strange lands filled with stranger people, which allowed them to experience the wider world—probably for the first and only time in their
lives. The pilgrims' constant sense of surprise and astonishment at the
ever-changing scenery, weather, and habits of others were as influen-
tial as the perils they had to overcome.

The commitment to visit the martyr's tomb in Santiago was but
the first step of an elaborately ritualized journey, one that mirrors the
great round that is the movement behind pilgrimage everywhere.
Departing pilgrims first sought out the special pilgrimage blessing of a
local priest. In those days, the journey to Rome, Santiago, or
Canterbury was considered so dangerous that it was uncertain
whether you would even return. Leaving on pilgrimage without a blessing was inconceivable, as was leaving without your affairs in order. A
letter called a *testimoniales* from the parish church enabled pilgrims to
avoid accusations of "adventuring" or "profiteering." With certificate
in hand, pilgrims would assemble the traditional costume: a broad-
brimmed hat, a scallop-shell badge indicating their passage, a satchel
worn across the back called an *escarcela*, or scrip, and a *bordon*, a "pilgrim's staff" or walking stick.

All sacred journeys are marked by ritual ceremony. The departing
pilgrims were celebrated with a Mass in which they took confession
and communion, then the rites of the blessing of their walking staffs,
satchels, and drinking gourds. Psalms were sung to "infuse courage

into the hearts" of the pilgrims, then they put on their long cloaks and hats, recited the prayers of the *Pilgrim's Itinerarium*, and set out with their fellow marchers down the long road.

THE GLORIOUS JOURNEY

The journey of a thousand miles begins with one step.
—Lao Tzu (570–490 B.C.E.)

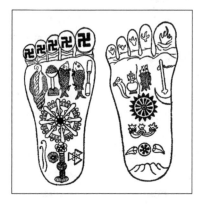

"*Buddha Foot Stones,*" *tracings from the T'ien-t'ai Monastery, Peiping, China. Etched into the footprints are religious emblems and auspicious symbols sacred to Buddhism.*

I began my pilgrimage on the first of January in 1953," wrote the remarkable woman who called herself the Peace Pilgrim. "It is my spiritual birthday of sorts. It was a period in which I was merged with the whole. No longer was I buried under the ground, but I felt as a flower reaching out effortlessly toward the sun. On that day I became a wanderer relying upon the goodness of others. It would be a pilgrim's journey undertaken in the traditional manner: on foot and on faith. I left behind all claims to a name, personal history, possessions and affiliations."

It would be a glorious journey.

For the next twenty-eight years, this woman with the peregrine spirit, who described herself simply as a "server in the world," walked around America from town to village, truck stop to school gymnasium, carrying her message of world peace. She stopped counting the miles in

1964, after more than 25,000, and never stopped her pilgrimage for peace until her untimely death in a car accident in 1982.

Jobless and penniless, Peace Pilgrim was not without support. Her faith allowed her to "press on, regardless," as Australians say. For eighteen years, she was irrepressible in her newsletter, *Pilgrim's Progress*. Her existence was lecturing, talking, and printing pamphlets; her only wish was to be remembered for her message of peace.

"A pilgrim is a wanderer with a purpose," she said. "A pilgrimage can be to a place—that's the best-known kind—but it can also be for a thing. Mine is for peace, and that is why I am a Peace Pilgrim." She thought of herself as the modern equivalent of the medieval pilgrim, sent out on the roads of the world without contributions or organizational backing. She believed herself to be "free as a bird," walking until offered shelter, fasting until offered food. "I don't ask—it's given without asking.... There's a spark of good in everybody, no matter how deeply it may be buried, it is there."

Her message constellated in her call, which came during, of all things, the Tournament of Roses Parade on January 1, 1953. At that moment, in the ancient tradition of pilgrims everywhere, she vowed "to remain a wanderer until mankind has learned the way to peace." From that time onward, she walked "as a prayer," wearing only her trademark "tunic," a blue sweatshirt stenciled on the front, with her name—*PEACE PILGRIM*—and her "mileage" on the back. Her worldly possessions consisted of nothing but a comb, a toothbrush, a ballpoint pen, handouts of her condensed message of peace to all who cared to hear, and her mail. Through the years, her pilgrimage embodied the old saying "the path is the goal." Her destinations, other than speaking engagements, were truck stops, parks, and radio and TV stations. She spoke out against the Korean War, the McCarthy witch hunt, the Vietnam War, and the nuclear arms race. Fearlessly, she walked where the brave usually dare not go, believing she was protected by her love of God and the goodness inherent in all strangers.

On that mythical morning of the Rose Parade, Peace Pilgrim simply walked ahead of the march, talking and handing out her message of
peace. Halfway along the parade route, a policeman approached her and
placed his hand on her shoulder.

"What we need," he said to her, "is thousands like you."

The woman known as Peace Pilgrim accomplished more than gaining forgiveness for her own or humanity's sins. She describes the way
she received the first "lesson" of her walking journeys: "I had been on
the giving side for many years and I needed to learn to accept as gracefully as I had been able to give, in order to give the other fellow the joy
and blessing of giving.

"I was tested severely in the beginning of my pilgrimage. Life is a
series of tests; but if you pass the tests, you look back upon them as
good experiences. . . .

"When I started out on my pilgrimage, I was using walking for two
purposes at that time. One was to contact people, and I still use it for
that purpose today. But the other was as a prayer discipline. To keep
me concentrating on my prayer for peace. And after a few years I discovered something. I discovered that I no longer needed the prayer discipline. I pray without ceasing now. . . .

"Concealed in every new situation we face is a spiritual lesson to be
learned and a spiritual blessing for us if we learn that lesson. It is good
to be tested. We grow and learn through passing tests. I look upon all
my tests as good experiences. . . . There is nothing that happens by
chance in our universe. Everything unfolds according to higher laws—
everything is regulated by divine order."

Her pilgrimage goes on. The Peace Pilgrim's books, based on her
many interviews, have sold more than 400,000 copies worldwide. An
organization inspired by her legacy continues to send out pamphlets
emblazoned with her message: a prayer for peace and the promise of
freedom.

"Think of how free I am," she said. "If I want to travel, I just stand up and walk away."

THE WAYFINDERS

You cannot travel the path until you have become the path.
—Gautama Buddha (563–483 B.C.E.)

In 1975, a young Hawaiian man named Nainoa Thompson had a vision that helped revive the ancient Polynesian art of long-distance navigation across the Pacific Ocean. Thompson sought out the last of the traditional navigators in Micronesia, Mau Piailug, to train him.

After nine months of work to ready him for a voyage to Tahiti, Mau led Nainoa to the lookout on the cliffs of the Big Island in Hawaii to study the patterns of the ocean waves. At sunset, Mau asked him to gaze out over the Pacific to the horizon and said, "Okay, point to Tahiti." Nainoa tried to picture it in his imagination, then figured it was safe to point in the general direction, "because you can't see it thousands of miles away."

Mau asked, "Do you see the island?"

Nainoa nervously replied that he could see the "image" of the island.

"Okay," his mentor replied. "If the wind goes this way, which way is the island going to move?" Mau was referring to the "star compass" Nainoa was being trained to imagine in his mind, as his ancestors had for centuries.

Nainoa pointed in the direction he thought it would move. Mau asked, "Okay, when the canoe goes this way, which way are the islands going to move and to what 'star house' would it go?" Once again, the apprentice pointed correctly.

Satisfied, Mau said, "Okay, you have the island in your mind, but if you lose it in your mind, you're lost."

That was Nainoa's final formal lesson. Mau said only, "Let's go home."

Only after memorizing the entire voyage in his mind, including variations due to wind, rain, storms, or lulls in the wind, was the young navigator ready to depart, to reenact the pilgrimage of his ancestors.

I heard this story when I was working on *Wayfinders: A Pacific Odyssey*, a PBS documentary film by Gail Evenari about the recent resurgence of traditional navigation among Pacific Islanders. I was struck by the beauty of the anecdote, the rigor of the training, the respect for the mentor relationship, but also by its similarity to my own intuitive method of departure. As with the Santiago pilgrims and the Peace Pilgrim, there is a poetic approach to the sacred journey, a highly developed picture of the goal—healing, rebirth, peace itself—that draws the traveler forward.

In the weeks before leaving on my own long journeys, I find it an exhilarating and challenging exercise to visualize the road unfolding ahead of me. Alternately, I feel like a painter contemplating the shock of white canvas, an author trying to imagine the finished book in the hand before setting pen to paper, or, as art lore would have it, the way Michelangelo was able to see the finished sculpture while gazing at unhewn marble. I imagine myself where I long to go: at Café Contrescarpe in Paris, canoeing upriver in the Amazon, walking the moors of Scotland, until I can see the destination in my mind's eye.

Then I ask myself: *Were you prepared for this moment?"*

This is what physicist Stephen Hawking calls "remembering the future."

Imagine how many ways you can prepare for your upcoming journey. Can you think of a way to ritualize your departure like the pilgrim who picks up her staff for the long walk to Santiago? Do you have a sacred cause, an unassailable purpose, like the pilgrim who marched for peace? Can you focus on your goal like a navigator about to embark on a ten-thousand-mile voyage?

Try to imagine that you are leaving for a journey from which you may never return. How would you "mark" the time? Would you hold a feast? Would you chronicle and record every moment? Rituals mark time, set space apart—two ways of defining what we mean by the sacred.

Before setting out, remind yourself of the *purpose* of your journey. From now on, there is no such thing as a neutral act, an empty thought, an aimless day. Travels become sacred by the depths of their contemplations. As in myth, dream, and poetry, every word is saturated with meaning.

Now is the time to live your ideal life.

THE WANDERING TIME

Glorious it is when wandering time is come.
—Eskimo song

Once the call for pilgrimage is heard, it is time to plan and clarify our intentions. Just as we had to be attentive to identify the source of our longing, it is now important for the traveler to be clear about the how and when of the journey. Some departures, like the Peace Pilgrim's, may seem dramatic and impetuous, but in truth hers had been gaining momentum for years through her work on local peace initiatives, in soup kitchens, and on environmental issues. When the moment arrived, it had a sense of inevitability. Each step she took in the journey she continued until the end of her life was made sacred by her indomitable spirit and clear sense of intention.

Before leaving on their sacred journeys, some Muslims prepare by shaving their head, trimming their nails, and donning an all-white

An Irish pilgrim on a tura, or circuit of holy wells and gravesites of Celtic saints, Donegal, Ireland.

pilgrim's robe. For others, it means the purifying rites of fasting, abstinence from sex, recitation of certain prayers, or contemplation of sacred texts. Among many Native American tribes, it is customary to stage a peyote or prayer meeting for a member of the tribe who is entering the military or college, or departing for a sundance ritual, peyote meeting, or a sacred pipe ceremony. To ready the soul for transition, the traveler prepares by fasting, abstention, and purification rituals.

The ancient Irish fasted and prayed before making the *turas*, the sacred rounds to the tombs of heroes and saints, where they might touch holy relics. When they reached the ruins of a medieval chapel or a cairn of megalithic stones, the pilgrims might leave behind a token offering of a rag, a nail, or some coins.

In his book *Aama in America: A Pilgrimage of the Heart*, Broughton Coburn tells how he befriended a diminutive, eighty-four-year-old Nepalese village woman named Vishnu Maya (Aama) when he lived in the Himalayas while working for the Peace Corps. After a longevity ceremony to honor her long life, he recalls the Hindu belief that "merit can be gained simply by undertaking a spiritual journey, especially if it is prolonged and hazardous." Thus inspired and authenticated, he takes Aama on a zigzagging twenty-five-state tour of America to help her "earn merit" for accomplishing an "end-of-life-pilgrimage," hoping that it might rejuvenate her. To prepare for such a momentous journey, Aama clenched blades of grass in her mouth, symbolizing the hair of Vishnu, knowing that it kept her from talking. Tradition had taught her that "she must not prolong the farewell nor gaze homeward once she walked from the doors of her house for the last time."

Imagine your departure as a metamorphosis. Through simple acts of intention and attention, you can transform even a sleepwalking trip into a soulful journey. The first step is to *slow down*. The next one is to treat everything that comes your way as part of the sacred time that envelops your pilgrimage.

THE PREPARATION

*The day on which one starts out is not the time
to start one's preparations.*
—Nigerian folk saying

Over the years, having talked with hundreds of people who are preparing for special journeys, I have come to realize that one reason so few prepare adequately for their travels is a reaction to the rigidity of their daily schedules at home. Mapping out dozens of deeply focused trips around the world has convinced me that preparation no more spoils the chance for spontaneity and serendipity than discipline ruins the opportunity for genuine self-expression in sports, acting, or the tea ceremony.

I also take solace in a remark made by Louis Pasteur after years of studying the phenomenon of serendipity in science: "In the field of observation, chance favors the prepared mind." My most memorable experiences on the road have come about because months or years of contemplation, reading, and journal-keeping had me alert enough to be ready for the moments that make travel worthwhile.

In their wonderful work *Pilgrims to the Holy Land*, Teddy Pollek and Moshe Perlman reprint the twenty-seven "articles" of rules of behavior that medieval pilgrims were expected to follow, as recorded by Felix Fabri. They include the following: "No pilgrim ought to wander alone about the holy places without a Saracen guide .... The pilgrim should be aware of stepping over the sepulchers of the Saracens.... Let the pilgrims beware of chipping off fragments from the Holy Sepulchers, and from the buildings at other places, and spoiling the hewn stones thereof.... Pilgrims must be aware of laughing together as they walk about Jerusalem to see the holy places, but they must be grave and devout...." The authors add that the twenty-seven articles were read aloud in Latin and German before the pilgrims were let off the ships, and so had "an immediate foretaste of the local attitude towards them...."

Articles in the Sunday *New York Times* travel section or in *Travel and Leisure* magazine are often about ongoing "culture clashes." These sources, together with great travel books, can help modern travelers find out about the strictures of behavior and customs of their destinations before leaving home, thus avoiding the kinds of confrontations that regularly occur on the steps of mosques, cathedrals, and synagogues the world over.

Anticipating another glitch in departures, author Alexander Eliot describes one of his family travel rituals as the "Russian way." After family members agree they've packed everything, they simply ... sit on their luggage for a half-hour. "It's a surefire way of leaving with peace of mind," he says. "If you've forgotten anything, it comes back to you as you sit there; if you've actually packed everything and taken care of your responsibilities, the extra time allows you to relax before setting off."

If you don't take the time to sit and reflect *before* you leave, you'll surely be remembering what you've forgotten when you're on the way to the airport or on the plane. By then it's too late. This tends to be true for what goes into your bags as well as what goes into your heart about the purpose of the journey.

Trish O'Rielly is a professional photographer and yoga instructor who lives in southern California. She has spent a great deal of time traveling in Europe, Asia, and India in both capacities. When she is ready to embark on a new journey, she prepares carefully, believing that intention is everything and that what she gets out of her travels is in direct proportion to how carefully and spiritually she prepares for them.

"I start to download a few days before leaving on an important journey," she explained after a recent trip to India. "For me, it's important to put everything in order before I leave. It's a sort of ritual. I have to touch every piece of paper, put them in the right place. When I leave I want to leave free, unencumbered. To do that means breaking the rhythm of what I'm doing at home. To really feel complete about leaving, I need to feel that when the door closes on the airplane or train, I have the ability to disconnect from the pressures, tasks, responsibilities of home."

Because her two pursuits both demand seeing and experiencing the world in depth, she takes seriously the need to enter another frame of mind. If she finds that she hasn't created a "a clear intent" before the departure, Trish will still have her "home" eyes, her ordinary sight, which is not enough, she insists, "on a sacred journey." To do this, she feels she has to isolate her intention with a combination of meditation, music, reading, and running.

"If my trip is going to be sacred, I need to *see* differently," she says. "I need to think new thoughts, not just conditioned responses. That's because I have a different relationship to time on the road, a freedom of thought I don't have at home—or don't allow myself at home, where I'm encumbered with relationships and responsibility."

For the past fifteen years, Michael Guillén has led groups into remote areas of Mexico, Guatemala, and Belize to share his passion for ancient architecture, Mayan epigraphy, and mythology. Because he works at a law firm in downtown San Francisco in his "other life," he has come to realize that he must "adjust himself" spiritually before leaving home.

"Before my sacred journeys, I pray!" he laughs. "It's the only time I pray. For the past few years I've prayed to a mysterious Mayan deity called Maximon, a syncretic god with ancient features and Christian ones. I also prepare by going over recent Mayan writings to see if there have been any recent decipherments I should know about.

"Mostly, I just pay closer attention. A departing pilgrim has to be attentive to the change he's going through, and that change begins the moment I commit to the new journey."

In the spirit of the trickster whose archetypal role is to help the student by killing pretension, scholar and theologian Rebecca Armstrong relishes Joseph Campbell's advice to a departing pilgrim one bitterly cold day in January 1972. Campbell had come to Chicago to give a lecture at the downtown YMCA. Armstrong's family had only recently established a tradition of offering him hospitality whenever he was in town, and Campbell would reciprocate by taking them out for steak dinner.

The heartiness of the beef bourguignon feast had improved everyone's spirits, and we fought our way cheerfully through the snow to the rather shabby WMCA on Grand. That evening he lectured to a small but enthusiastic audience on the nature of the goddess, concluding with a brief homily on the role of the artist in society and the need of our times for more women poets. His words brought radiant smiles to the faces of the two published female poets in his audience, of whose presence he was not unaware! After the lecture he was besieged by those who had pressing individual questions for him. He listened and answered graciously to all. I was lingering nearby, still trying to digest the immense ideas from his lecture as well as the remainder of the beef dinner, and overheard the following encounter. A woman in her late thirties or early forties approached Joe and, speaking very rapidly, with great emotion began to outline her plan for going to Greece to "find the spirit of the goddess that you spoke of tonight." She pulled out a notebook and showed Joe her itinerary. She had made precise calculations of the best times to visit every major cultural attraction and just where and when she would make her salutations to the various deities whose statues remained. "Do you think this is sufficient?" she pressed Joe. "Do you think I'll find the spirit of the goddess?"

Joe had been staring at her while a parade of mixed emotions played over his features. Now he took her one free hand in his and with great kindness and solemnity said, "Dear lady, I sincerely hope that all does not go as planned."

With that, he slipped into his overcoat and we left the building. Sitting in the backseat of the car on the drive home, I could barely contain my curiosity. Finally, mustering all the courage of my seventeen years, I leaned over the front seat and said, "Mr. Campbell, that woman who was going to Greece—why did you tell her that you hoped things did not go as planned?" Joe paused as if trying to sort through all the encounters of the evening, and then threw back his head and laughed with a mystic's glee. "How will the gods ever find her when she has done everything in her power to make sure that they never will?!" he exclaimed. Then, very soberly: "Unless you leave room for serendipity, how can the divine enter in? The beginning of the adventure of finding yourself is to lose your way!"

The conversation then turned to other topics, but I sat back relish-
ing this insight from the master mythologist. It is a piece of advice
I have never forgotten and in all my travels I try to leave a space
for serendipity—how else will the gods find me?

THE BLESSING

Give Thy blessing, we pray Thee, to our daily work,
that we may do it in faith, and heartily.
—Thomas Arnold (1795–1842)

My rituals for travel preparation include a ceremonial meal before leaving and a ritual phone call to one of my esteemed elders. Before departing for Paris in 1987, I called Professor Campbell to wish him well with his work on his *Historical Atlas of World Mythology* and to simply evoke what was for both of us our favorite city. His voice took on a shimmer of delight as we talked about his years in Paris in the late 1920s, his friendship with Sylvia Beach, his discovery of modern art. His hearty *bon voyage* felt like a blessing.

On the eve of my departure for the Philippines in 1981, I rang up a friend who had been stationed there during the Vietnam War. Before my 1993 Amazon adventure, Robert A. Johnson, who first made me promise to be careful and take care of myself, then told me a marvelous parable about a dangerous journey he once took on a fourth-class train across India. In his own way, Robert was giving me the nod of approval that there are young men's journeys and old men's journeys.

Each of these conversations helped me focus on the upcoming journey and lent each of them a pleasant weight. For me, they acknowl-edged the ancient belief that I would not be alone on my travels if I had the blessing of an elder.

PACKING THE SATCHEL

Behold a man clothed in Rags, standing at a certain place,
with his face from his own house, A Book in his hand,
and a great Burden on his back....
—John Bunyan, *Pilgrim's Progress*

B eing ready mentally, spiritually, and physically makes us lighter
on our feet, more adroit at making decisions, and perhaps can
even help keep chaos at bay. Bearing in mind that the journey to come
might turn out to be our first deeply significant pilgrimage puts the
entire trip in a different context. Being alert to the possibility that it
could also be our last journey—accidents do occur—or that when we
return we might face financial ruin and not travel again for years can
sober us very quickly about the supposed ease of travel. One of the
soulful questions to ask ourselves as we are poised to leave is: What
can I do to lighten my burden on this journey?

How we pack our bags defines our journey. We always have a
choice. I was given the wonderful gift of a beautiful Swedish leather
satchel in Paris in the late 1980s, so I am personally touched by the
images of the thin leather satchel that Santiago pilgrims carried over
their shoulder, or the simple backpack that Japanese pilgrims traditionally wore. The venerable tradition of traveling with one satchel or
bag symbolizes the fundamental philosophy of pilgrimage: *Simplicity,*
simplicity, simplicity! As Thoreau learned from his sojourn at Walden
Pond:

> *I say, let your affairs be as two or three, and not a hundred or a*
> *thousand; instead of a million count half a dozen, and keep your*
> *accounts on your thumb-nail.... Simplify, simplify, simplify.*

In *Tracking the Serpent,* Janine Pommie Vega tells how a lover once invited her to visit him in Spain, requesting her only to bring two things that she loved. What a soulful invitation that is, truly the spirit of pilgrimage, reflecting the power of a talisman. My personal talismans include candles for ritual lightings to honor family and friends, a canvas hat, a walking stick, a favorite stone my father gave me from a trip he took to his grandfather's farm in Ontario, and a Zuni fetish—a beautiful tawny cougar that fits into the palm of my hand—which was presented to me at Canyon de Chelly, in Arizona. It's remarkable how literally "handling" an item like this can evoke vivid emotional and grounding memories.

The pilgrim's staff is unnecessary for city travels but is indispensable for long walking tours. I have a collection of walking sticks I've brought back from my journeys, including a twisting serpentine stick from the Philippines and a shillelagh from Ireland. Along with being eminently practical to keep balance, I find that they are also deeply contemplative beings to have along with me: Each moment it touches the ground, the staff reminds me that I'm treading the maze into sacred land. If it's impractical to carry a walking stick on your journey, an alternative is to remember to walk barefoot at least once a day. There is something quite satisfying about taking off your shoes and socks and feeling the earth under your feet when you are in a strange land.

For my long journeys, I take a woven *kilim* bag I bought in the Grand Bazaar of Istanbul. Because it has only two end pockets and one interior space, I'm forced to severely limit what I carry. My satchel holds my writing journal, cameras, sketch pad, pencils and watercolors, letter-writing paper, *blank* postcards (I make my own drawings on them for a personal touch), mini-binoculars, guidebooks, and language dictionaries. On every journey, in addition to a local guidebook and phrase book, I also bring along at least two other books—biography and poetry—that, for me, condenses and compresses the soul of a culture. On a recent trip to St. Petersburg, Russia, I carried a

One of the time-tested methods for practicing how to see for yourself on a long journey is simple sketching. Here are three drawings from my travel journals: a farmhouse on Guernsey; the ancient menhirs of Carnac, France; and the ambling James Joyce (after Harmsworth).

biography of the poet Anna Akmatova; on an expedition into the Guatemalan rain forest, I carried the journals of archaeologist James Stephens; to South America, I carried a beautiful edition of *Odes to Ordinary Things* by Pablo Neruda. Reading others who have gone the way we are about to sets the stage, gives a frame, provides a context for our upcoming travels.

But books are heavy to carry in abundance. Because weight is one the greatest burdens to the pilgrim, one way to stay in touch with sacred writing is to "make your own Bible," as Emerson suggested. Collect favorite writings, from poetry to parables, short stories to historical references, that are most deeply moving *to you* and create your own "Book of Hours." This is easily done by purchasing an open-bound "page holder," the kind that holds manuscripts, and fill it with photo-copied pages or passages you've written out *by hand*. This practice reflects an ancient belief that anything done by hand is a sacred act.

This has been a valuable discovery for me. Each morning before setting off—through the cobbled streets of Prague, on the sandy shores of Paros in the Mediterranean, among the rice terraces of the Philippines, wherever I may be—I reread the lines of favorite authors, poets, songwriters, naturalists, cosmologists, and ancient travelers, and let them hover above me for the rest of the day. In this way, I choose what will be drifting around in my mind when I relax, rather than be "victimized" by goofy jingles from childhood or bad movie dialogue that seeps in from the great projectors in the sky. Thus prepared, I feel as if I'm ready for any contingency—plane delay, traffic jam in the taxi, rainy days on-site, lazy café afternoons—to be inspired by more than old newspapers or the prosaic, albeit useful, guidebook.

This is a form of meditation for me, in the spirit of Emily Dickinson, who described prayer simply as "night descended upon thought." While traveling, at least once a day what I think of as *the mood* descends over me. The *brooding* begins, feelings I don't like to slough off because I sense my soul coming alive. When the "pilgrim mood" descends upon me, I open my journal or sketchbook, or a favorite book of poetry, or my photocopied pages.

Here are some lines from my journals:

> *Perhaps to assuage the fears of those of his followers afraid to leave on a long journey, or speaking metaphorically of the spiri-tual quest, the thirteenth-century Sufi mystic Rumi said, "As you start on the Way, the Way appears."*

> *"The Wayless Way," said Meister Eckhart, "where the Sons of God lose themselves and, at the same time, find themselves."*

Our word "journey" derives from the French word for day,
"jour," hence the distance traveled in one day. In turn, the word
"progress" devolved from "journey" in Middle English, more
specifically "seasonal journey" or "circuit."

When a monk asked, "What is the Tao?" Master Ummon
replied, "Walk on."

THE SACRED CIRCLE

Everything sacred moves in a circle.
—Black Elk

After an all-night peyote ceremony high in the mountains of
northern Mexico, my old friend, the Winnebago holy man
Reuben Snake, told me why Indians don't like straight lines. "To us,
everything important in life is a circle. A holy mystery comes our way,
surrounds us. We better be ready—or it will pass us by." He then
pointed at a group of Tarahumara Indians who had run 250 miles in
tire-tread sandals to participate in the ceremony with us. "Now look at
our brothers and sisters there. They believe so deeply in that mystery
that they fasted for four days before they left on their holy journey
because they wanted to be worthy of the vision that was waiting for
them here."

At the time, I thought of the prophetic lines of Black Elk, whose
vision of the sacred universe encompassed the notion that the center
was everywhere. But he also saw that the sacred hoop of life had been
tragically broken and prophesized that it would take seven generations
for that circle to be mended. His descendants are currently making
that vision come true with their revival of tribal ways.

Yet it is also true that the sacred circle is in a perpetual state of being broken, and it is the function of art, religion, philosophy, ritual, and dreams to heal that rupture. This is why the complete circle is a universal symbol for the soul—an image of wholeness—and the goal of the sacred journey is to become as whole again as possible. Our longing is the sign that there is a gap in the circle. Our life burns with the desire to complete the circuit with our journey.

First described by the Dutch anthropologist Arnold van Gennep, the universal rite of passage consists of three stages: *separation, ordeal,* and *reintegration.* The cycle suggests that each movement from one life stage to another demands a break from the past, the enduring of an ordeal, and then a return to ordinary life. In Joseph Campbell's model of the hero's journey, or monomyth, the sequence goes: *separation, initiation, return.* In William Melczer's view, pilgrimage, like ritual processions to churches, synagogues, or mosques, is a *progression* that moves in a circle. "One comes in order to return, not in order to stay; one fills oneself with the sacredness transpiring from the relics and one departs home." In this observation, the pilgrim's cycle replays nature's pattern of regeneration, a journey consisting of *departure, arrival,* and *return.* The pattern may be deeply ingrained but it still requires vision and courage. According to an old Hasidic saying, "Carefully observe the way your heart draws you and then choose that way with all your strength."

"We are all pilgrims on our own quests, like it or not," novelist Robert Stone has written, "deny it or not. The structure of life is so."

The impact James Joyce's book *Portrait of the Artist as a Young Man* had on me one night when I reached rock-bottom in my travels around Ireland is impossible to describe. Joyce's protagonist Stephen Daedalus braces himself with courage as he sets out from the shores of Ireland to make the writer's pilgrimage to Paris: "Welcome, O life! I go to encounter for the millionth time the reality of experience and to forge in the smithy of my soul the uncreated conscience of my race."

Reimagine the yearning in your heart for a transformative journey, such as that for the natural world Basho expressed when he set out for the far provinces, saying, "There came a day when the clouds drifting along with the wind aroused a wanderlust in me, and I set off on a journey to roam along the seashores...."

THE THRESHOLD

What do you have that can get past them?
—Robert Bly

Once prepared on the outside through packing and on the inside through prayers, songs, and blessings, you are ready to cross the threshold. The threshold is more than an architectural detail; it is a mythological image that evokes the spirit of resistance we must pass through on our risky journey from all we've known to all that's unknown. It is the first step toward renewal. The truth of the image is compressed into the word. *Threshold* comes from *threshing*, what was done to separate the seed from the chaff right on the entrance to the farmhouses. Since at least Roman times, the threshold is "the slab or bar at the main doorway that prevents water or mud flowing into the house." The threshold divides the inside from the outside, the sacred from the profane, the past from the future.

Crossing over means confronting the guardian at the gate, the personification of the forces trying to keep us in the village, the ordinary world. The sheer ferociousness of those guardians, such as the ones at the Todai-ji Temple in Nara, Japan, are also personifications of our fear as we anticipate leaving on a meaningful journey. A vacation is easy to

A local farmer stands guard at the entrance of a four-thousand-year-old megalithic tomb on Guernsey, in the Channel Islands. He tells visitors he goes to the site each morning to stand "in touch" with his ancestors.

embark upon; everything has been laid out for us to have a predictable, comfortable, and reassuring holiday. But a pilgrimage is different; we are actually beckoning to the darkness in our lives. The fear is real.

Muriel Rukeyser, in her magnificent essay *The Life of Poetry*, writes of something I find perfectly analogous to the situation of the departing traveler. She is concerned—baffled—by the resistance of people to poetry. She finds that most of them claim to be turned off by the obscurity or difficulty of modern poetry, yet would be drawn to the obscurity in science or even painting and music.

"This resistance has the quality of fear, it expresses the fear of poetry.... A poem invites you to feel. More than that: it invites you to respond. And better than that: a poem invites a total response.... A fine poem will seize your imagination intellectually—that is, when you reach it, you will reach it intellectually too—but the way is through emotion, through what we call feeling."

So too with powerful and soulful travel. It seizes your imagination, but the way through to the sacred moment can also be through deep anxiety about the unknown. That possibility produces fear in many travelers, even at the threshold of their own door before leaving home. The lion's roar, the fire of the dragon, the master's hand slap—all are different ways of expressing the same thing: the call to *wake up*.

What is the threshold guardian waiting for?

A gift.

When you leave home, you are a stranger, and a stranger is always feared. That is why the wise traveler carries gifts. To make a peace offering at every stop of a pilgrimage is to recognize the sacred nature of the journey with a deep personal purpose.

If you listen hard, you can hear the ancient advice: *Pass by whatever you do not love.*

Imagine the moment of departure as the crossing of a threshold. The anxiety you may feel is the reverse of the thrill of anticipation. Something new is about to happen; something unexpected but transformative. As you plan your leavetaking, consider what you might offer at the shrines you plan to visit. The shift from the tourist emphasis on "taking photographs," "taking souvenirs home," "taking a break," to "leaving" something behind is the pilgrim move. A walk around an old Celtic cross or holy well in Ireland is an astonishment: Bright white flags flutter in the air, gestures from pilgrims that they, indeed, had been there. Coins dropped into a fountain or well or poorbox, letters left behind at a national park office for the goddess of the volcano, pencils and postcards of your hometown left behind for beggar children rather than candy or cigarettes—all are simple "gratitudes," acts of gratitude that you have been blessed with on this journey. Ask yourself what *your* gratitudes will be *before* you leave. Keep one pocket in your satchel just for these.

An eighteenth-century illustration of two travelers visiting the
dolmen at Proleek, Ireland.

When he lived in the Greek Islands, poet Jack Gilbert made a ritual of giving thanks. In *Monolithos*, he writes:

To the arriving and leaving. To the journey
I wake to the freshness. And do reverence.

One blustery day in County Clare, Ireland, I set off for a day's hike
to see the ancient dolmens and Celtic crosses. The rain was slashing in
from the Atlantic sideways. I leaned forward, hand on my tweed cap, to
keep from being blown over.

A farmer was leaning against his hoe in a small garden, enjoying the
storm. Before I could say anything, he asked, "Aye, lad, are you going
to the stones?"

I nodded, shivering but bemused. It was an ancient greeting in
these parts. He looked cursorily at the accordioned map in my shivering hands, then shook his head in dismay and gazed out over the
windswept burren. I asked him where the road led that passed his old
thatched-roof house.

"To the end, lad," he replied slowly, "to the end."

I set off alone but confident, the map trembling in my hands, a thrill of anticipation in my heart. Ahead of me loomed stone graves that had drawn travelers like me for 4,000 years. My life was not diminished by that perspective; it was widened. Something was pulling me here. The Poulnabrone dolmen slanted against the gray-slate sky, water running off it in rivulets. I thought about the force that inspired men and women to raise these monuments, the belief that the sacred is not an idea, but a force in life.

For an hour, I huddled underneath the huge roof of the dolmen, sketching, reading Yeats, thrumming to the moment. I thought of how the old Irish called a pilgrim *gyrovagus*, a "gyrating wanderer." The idea of a "Celtic whirling dervish" spinning from one pilgrimage site to another came to mind and I smiled and thought, *This is where I am supposed to be.*

A second task once you have crossed the threshold is to listen intently to everything around you. A pilgrimage is an opportunity to reconnect with your soul. But that is difficult if the radio frequency is jammed. Solitudinous time listening to music is a remarkably effective way to get back into the habit of listening closely when traveling. Ask yourself when was the last time you felt true joy after a conversation with someone. Become aware of how closely you listen to your friends, family, even the radio when it is playing. Chances are if you are not listening now it will be difficult to simply switch on once you are traveling. Begin now.

Finally, now is the time to begin your pilgrimage journal. Find the silent part of your day, whether early in the morning when everyone else is asleep, or late at night when the city is quiet. Recollection is an effective way to illuminate your true motivation. Recall past journeys, incomplete journeys. Write about whatever comes to mind as your pilgrimage constellates in your imagination.

Imagine the last time you truly listened. What are you listening for now? What calls do you hear amid the cacophony of your life? What are you praying for? Recall that inside every question is a quest trying to get out. To get to the question, you have to get out.

As author Martin Palmer said, "True pilgrimage changes lives, whether we go halfway around the world or out to our own backyards." Whether you are embarking on a grueling walking pilgrimage a thousand miles across Europe to a famous shrine, setting off on the long-delayed journey to your ancestral roots, or taking that first step on the long spiritual journey into a creative project, your journey is about to change you.

If that isn't worth chronicling, what is?

IV
THE PILGRIM'S WAY

Does the road wind uphill all the way?
Yes, to the very end.
Will the journey take the whole long day?
From morn to night, my friend.

—Christina Rossetti, 1867

IN THE EARLY 1980S, CHINA GALLAND SET OUT ON A SERIES of pilgrimages to many sacred sites around the world to explore the meaning of "the darkness within darkness" embodied in the strange and marvelous images of Tara and the Black Madonna. After venturing through India, Nepal, Switzerland, and France, she reached Poland in August 1987 to participate in a two-week-long pilgrimage to the shrine of Our Lady of Czestochowa at the Jasna Gora Monastery. In Warsaw, she and 35,000 others—hundreds of groups of pilgrims from churches all around the city—set out to march thirty kilometers a day. By the time they reached the monastery, nearly a million pilgrims would converge in one massive show of faith.

In her exhilarating book *Longing for Darkness*, Galland explains that the Paulines were responsible for the care of the Black Madonna at Jasna Gora ("Mountain of Light") when Ladislaus, the Duke of Opole, brought them to Czestochowa from Hungary in the fourteenth century. "One of their members," she writes, "initiated this pilgrimage from Warsaw 276 years ago when the city was filled with plague. The Pauline fathers have kept the pilgrimage going each year, no matter what wars, famine, or governments, including those of Hitler and Krushchev, have arisen to stop it."

On the march itself, Galland was moved by the rituals of the rosary, the presentation of flowers and songs to priests and nuns, and the frequency of shrines along the road to the Black Madonna, which reminded her of shrines she had seen in the Himalayas. Although she had trained at home for the grueling walk, by the second day her feet were blistered and bandaged from toe to ankle. A nurse told her that

Pilgrims from all over the Baltic states venture to the Gate of Dawn, in Vilnius, Lithuania, to pray to the Icon of the Virgin, a dark-skinned, gold-clad image of the Madonna reputed to have miraculous powers.

she should take a break from the pilgrimage, but Galland persisted. On the third day, she began to weave in and out of reverie, praying, meditating, and singing. She found walking the great distances to be spiritual practice, despite the pain. She found solace in Thich Nhat Hanh's advice to "Take refuge in the present moment."

Along the route, worn down and "stripped emotionally," she became suspicious of police informants. But near the end of the march, nine kilometers from the shrine, her group halted along the road for a ceremony of forgiveness called *Przepraszam*. She was told that it is customary to approach anyone whom you may have offended or hurt during the pilgrimage and express your apologies, saying "*Przepraszam*," which also expresses, "I'm sorry, please forgive me for anything I may have done to hurt you." She found a young man she had been impatient with, said her "*Przepraszam*," and felt cleansed and revitalized for the journey.

When they converged on Czestochowa, the pilgrimage wound down slowly. Hours later, Galland was inside the monastery and with a final push approached the icon of the Black Madonna at the end of the chapel. Slowly she inched nearer, but could only catch a fleeting glimpse of the icon because of the crush of fellow pilgrims. Enshrined, the Madonna was surrounded by amulets, necklaces, rosaries, crutches, "stunning in her silver and jewels, set into the black altar," as she describes it. "And yet so remote! I cannot begin to fathom this image...."

In each of us dwells a pilgrim. It is the part of us that longs to have direct contact with the sacred. We will travel halfway around the world and endure great sacrifice and pain to enter the sanctuary, whether it is a temple, shrine, cemetery, or library. This is the way that is no way, but a practice.

"It's not so much *what* you do," wrote Epictetus in his study of happiness, "it's *how* you do it."

Your practice *is* your path. If so, "The Way is uncontrived," as Lao Tzu said. It is simply the way of seeing, the way of hearing, the way of touching, the way of walking, the way of being, with humility.

THE WAY OF THE SACRED

Here we must deal with awe, fascination, and terror,
with ignorance shot through with the lightning of certainty,
and with feelings of exuberance, love and bliss....
—Francis Huxley

Whether by walking or by traveling via plane, ship, train, bicycle, or bus, the pilgrim progresses across time as well as space. The ambitiousness of the goal, the intensity of devotion ensure that the sight of new landscapes, the smell of novel foods, the encounter with unusual customs—all converge to create a new way of experiencing the world. The legendary hospitality and deference afforded pilgrims also contributes to the sense of delight and gratitude for the unfolding adventure.

All around the world, millions of people set out on meandering roads to make a connection with something they believe to be holy and sacred. Early pilgrimages to sacred sites in Mesopotamia, Egypt, Africa, and to *tabu* islands in the Pacific are largely unrecorded, though there are echoes of the tradition in old myths and legends. There was once a vast network of sea passages to sacred Greek islands, the blessed isle of Apollo and Diana's birth at Delos, which was so sacred that people could visit only during the day, and births and deaths on the island were forbidden. Ancient travelers visited the slopes of the mountains on Crete where Zeus was born, and the gorges of Mount Parnassus where the Sibyls ruled until Delphi was ordained for the Oracle of Apollo.

Throughout old Ireland, pilgrim roads existed for the heavy traffic of supplicants pursuing the veneration of saints at ancient tombs and chapels. With the legendary discovery by Constantine's mother, Helena, of the True Cross in Jerusalem, in 326 C.E., the practice of following in the footsteps of the Savior was inaugurated, and it has continued unabated to the present day. Any traveler to India is well aware of the omnipresence of pilgrims at every holy site; an estimated 20 million pilgrims visit the 1,800 Hindu shrines each year. According to legend, the relics of the Buddha were scattered to 84,000 stupas, a mythical number indicating that his life perfectly reflected the length of the *yugas*, the cosmic ages. But the number is also a poetic image suggesting that the Buddha is everywhere, and so pilgrimage is always possible. Medieval Europe was webbed with pilgrimage roads. Today those roads are still thronged. There are 6,000 recognized pilgrimage roads in western Europe alone, not counting the secular versions such as museums and shrines of famous artists.

Everywhere, the way of the pilgrim is twofold, exterior and interior, the simultaneous movement of the feet and the soul through time as well as space. This dual role is epitomized in the tradition of sacred travel in Tibet.

"Pilgrimage comes naturally to the Tibetans, a people characterized by movement," writes Edwin Bernbaum in *The Encyclopedia of Religion*. Tibetan practice is realized in the ritual circling of mountains, a time-tested method of devotion that has come from Indian Buddhism, "where it began as a means of paying homage to a sacred person or object." The word *gnas-skor* means "circumambulation to a sacred place," Bernbaum explains. "The great round from departure to turning homeward is considered the larger circle of circumambulation within which wheel around the smaller circuits."

For these journeys, short guidebooks called *dkar chag* have been used for centuries and include details of entire pilgrimage networks and guides to "such legendary places as the hidden kingdom of Shambhala" and other sites such as towns and monasteries, sacred caves, springs, lakes, and mountains.

The purpose of Tibetan pilgrimage includes receiving spiritual and material blessings from sacred objects, persons, shrines, and places; obtaining teachings and initiations from spiritual masters; and leaving offerings. Tibetan practice reflects the art of contemplative travel, but why do we go to the mountain?

In his book *Sacred Mountains*, Bernbaum describes the confluence between the symbolism of holy mountains and the impulse to pilgrimage: "The sense of the sacred awakened by mountains reveals a reality that has the power to transform lives. Whatever that reality is ... a deity, the ground of being, emptiness, the unconscious, the self, nature, the absolute—our encounter with it frees us from our usual conceptions.... By awakening a sense of the sacred, making us aware of a deeper reality, mountains connect us to the world and make our lives more real."

In these inspired words, Bernbaum condenses centuries of devout practice around the world. We make our way across strange landscapes to be in the presence of an icon or a mountain because there is a compass rose of the spirit within us that points in that direction and a voice that beckons us. That inner voice, or perhaps the voices of elders or poets or prophets, echoes down through the ages, reminding us that an encounter with the sacred, the *wholly other*, the inscrutable mystery that is visible only to the eyes of the heart can, as Bernbaum writes, "overturn old conceptions and awaken a new awareness."

The pilgrim deep within us longs to be seized in this grasp, not only for the pleasure of the moment, but for the rare joy that can be brought back with us. "Climb the mountains and receive their glad tidings," as John Muir said.

"The contemplation of sacred mountains," Bernbaum reminds us, "with their special power to awaken another, deeper way of experiencing reality, opens us to a sense of the sacred in our own homes and communities—a sense that we need to cultivate in order to live in harmony."

Pilgrimage is often regarded as the universal quest for the self. Though the form of the path changes from culture to culture, through different epochs of history, one element remains the same: renewal of the soul. The shape can be linear, as with the goal-oriented journeys to Mecca or Rome; circular, as on the island route of Shikoku, Japan; or spiral, as in many mountain ascents. For the wandering poet like Basho, pilgrimage was a journey that embodied the essentials of Zen, a simple journey in which the path was the goal, yet also a spiritual metaphor for the well-lived life.

The purpose of the pilgrimage is to make life more meaningful. Through sacred travel, individuals can find the path to the divine, the ultimate source of life. The essence of the sacred way is "tracing a sacred route of tests and trials, ordeals and obstacles, to arrive at a holy place and attempt to fathom the secrets of its power." As Francis Huxley points out in *The Sacred*, it is precisely through the sharing of this sacred territory that people have come not only to discover the *idea* of their origins and their destiny, but to have *experiences* of it that reveal the meaning of their lives. "The sacred itself is plainly a mystery of consciousness," he writes, "using the word *mystery* to signify not a problem that can be intellectually solved, but a process of awakening and transformation that must be acted out in order to be experienced, and experienced if one is to make it one's own."

Stories such as that of Moses and the burning bush, or Arjuna beholding the vision of Krishna, or James Joyce's bittersweet epiphanies in his short-story collection *The Dead*, are invaluable because they give us hints—not exact directions—to that liminal place where revelations take place.

Although for a few pilgrims "the act of simply wandering (no matter if the destination is known or not) is enough," writes Martin Robinson, "for most, the sense of treading ground made holy by past events is crucial ... to sense in the numinous realm an atmosphere of awe and wonder ... an immediate sense of the holy.... The experience of the pilgrim in actually walking in the way of others enables them to become a participant in all that has happened. The pilgrim becomes one with all who have gone before."

For many travelers, the intention may have more than one dimension. Hillaire Belloc describes his walk between St. Cloud, France and Rome in his classic 1902 book *The Path to Rome*. "It is, of course," comments Michael Novak, "just as it announces itself, a delicious revel in the simple pleasures of the Moselle, the Alps, and Tuscany, upon the long path toward primal Western origins in central Italy.... The voyage, though, is inward. It is not an artist's tour, or archaeologist's, or antiquarian. Belloc pays little homage to the great cities, the famous monuments, or works of art along the way. He chooses to celebrate rather the way of life of the little people, not the sites beloved of tour books."

Novak's other insight into Belloc's much-beloved path, what he called "the strange light of adventure," is instructive for modern travelers. Belloc's pilgrimage to Rome, that treasure trove of relics, was also a "meditative journey" designed to "store up intellectual energy necessary for a life's work."

Welsh writer Edward Thomas' haunting story "A Pilgrim" tells of an anonymous man walking what was long called The Dark Lane, the ancient pilgrims' track between Cardigan and St. David's, in Wales. Alongside the road, he encounters a mysterious young man (who, he imagines, is a poet who supports himself with prose), carving a pilgrim's cross into a stone.

Without being asked why, the *poet manqué* explains that all the therapy and literature in the world have not helped him through his life crisis, but that he had come to respect what pilgrims had to endure to reach a shrine such as St. David's, which did not even exist anymore. He simply admired the way they kept their faith. The troubled youth tells the narrator that he wanted to carve a pilgrim's cross in stone in the hopes of knowing how a pilgrim feels when enduring a pilgrimage.

The conclusion to Thomas' story is open-ended, as many strange encounters are. Is it vainglorious to think that miming another's action can help us see into his heart, help us *feel* like him? Or are we to believe that there is a homeopathic principle involved in ritual?

I see the troubled narrator watch the dispirited youth chisel away at the old stone, blow by blow, until the sun goes down, then run his fingers through the incised cross, trying to imagine what it means to practice something, even faith, long enough to learn it by heart.

In sacred travel, every experience is uncanny. No encounter is without meaning. There are signs everywhere, if only we learn how to read them. In "A Pilgrim," the narrator can choose to regard the neo-pilgrim on the road as just peculiar or as a messenger. So can we each time we meet a stranger—or even strange behavior—on the road.

"From now," advised Epictetus, "practice saying to everything that appears unpleasant: 'You are just an appearance and by no means what you appear to be.'" Use the powers of your sacred imagination, the old Roman sage is saying. See behind the veil of things. Everything matters along the road, but what matters *deeply* is what is invisible and must be seen with the inner eye.

I encountered a marvelous example of this in the summer of 1997 at an art exhibition from Angkor Wat at the Grand Palais in Paris. It was an ineffably beautiful show of the glorious legacy of Khmer sculpture. There were maps and photographs of the "Khmer Ganges," the sacred river and inland sea leading to Angkor Wat, statues of the Bodhisattva Avalokiteshvara, and ornate sandstone pediment sculptures of sensuous *apsaras* and flying *garudas*. But the focus of the show was a serene bust of Jayavarman VII, the reigning king during the golden age of the Khmers. So preternaturally contemplative was the exquisite piece that the crowd surrounded it and moved around it as if in ritual circumambulation.

One man in particular caught my eye, an elderly, elegantly dressed, white-bearded Frenchman. He moved back and forth in front of the sculpture, enraptured. Every few seconds, he would glance down at a small notebook in his hands and write down an observation, like a man in love. After a while, I found myself looking closer at the sculpture. Magically, my own gaze began to intensify, my appreciation deepen. I felt myself transported back to Angkor, trying to imagine how the king had managed to find serenity in a time of such turbulence.

As unobtrusively as possible, I followed the Frenchman for several steps. In his notebook were short phrases and verses, each word written after a single glance at the stone head. The rhythm of his glances was metrical, musical: look, write; look, write; look, write. Those words were drawn with as much care and deliberation as any artist creating a still life.

He was sketching poetry.

This was no mere visit to a museum.

Imagine once again the goal of your journey. What is your *way?* How do you see yourself wending your way there? In what way are you walking? As a tourist in search of entertainment? A nomad adrift? An explorer?

In ancient Sanskrit, the word for chess player was the same as that for pilgrim. Try to see yourself on a chess board.

What is your next move?

THE WAY OF SEEING

We usually don't look, we overlook.
—Alan Watts

If there is a trick to soulful travel, it is learning to see for yourself. To do this takes practice and a belief that it matters. The difference between pilgrim and tourist is the intention of attention, the quality of the curiosity.

Rilke's letters to his wife on the week he spent gazing at the paintings of Paul Cézanne in Paris at the turn of the century are equivalent to still-life paintings. This was not a case of a reporter being dispatched to a gallery to report on the daubings of someone already famous, but the result of personal discovery, of Rilke's experience of being ineffably moved by a single painter on a single day, and compelled to return again and again afterward to *deepen* his understanding, his very perception.

The traveler soon learns that it is difficult to unlearn a lifetime of habitual seeing, the ordinary perception that gets one through a day at home but is inadequate to the task of comprehending the suddenly unfamiliar, strange, even marvelous things. Mort Rosenblum faces this situation frequently as a foreign correspondent. He has come to believe that reporting is "figurative pilgrimage." He has to go to the "source" of every story if he is going to discover the truth.

"You find who the goddess or god is in every story, whether it's about the crumbling of the Soviet Union, the old slave markets of Africa, or the new restaurant in France being opened by Alice Waters. It's a constant. You go to the roots, the sources. When I wrote *The Secret Life of the Seine*, that's what I had to do—go to the source, which turned out to be three rivulets—a wellspring that becomes a mighty river." He appreciates the metaphor of the pilgrimage being a journey with a purpose. "I'm like a pilgrim who's *got* to see things for himself. When the imagination is fired, the soul follows."

In his classic book *A Holy Tradition of Working*, Eric Gill writes: "It's man's special gift to know holiness."

"How do we *know* that gift?" he asks. By striving to know how to use the imagination. He illustrates his point with the image of the Greek sculptor using his imagination more than his sight. "Instead of saying 'seeing is believing,'" writes Gill: "'To believe is to see.'"

The artist and pilgrim, soulful travelers in parallel realms, are by nature similar; like Siamese twins, they are connected by the tissue of desire to experience the world directly. The pilgrim is a poetic traveler, one who believes that there is poetry on the road, at the heart of everything. Soulful travel is the art of finding beauty even in ruins, even in inclement weather, even in foul moods. Like art, pilgrimage cannot wait for the right mood to appear. Like poetry, pilgrimage is beyond time and space. It happens now, or it doesn't happen at all. To allow room for surprise and improvisation is to begin the apprenticeship of learning the way that is no way.

For Joan Marler, scholar and biographer of Marija Gimbutas and tour leader to sacred goddess sites, proper preparation must carry on moment by moment during the actual journey. She encourages her tour participants to do this by asking them to view their decision to go on the sacred journey as being similar to seeing through a new aperture: "I always see things on a metaphysical or mythological level—so I try to travel with minimal motivation, not too much interference, just a new perspective. But that is enough, because a new outlook can lead to a realignment of intuition

One of the pleasures of "ruin-hunting," as antiquarians call it, is discovering the beauty of small details. Note the "Knot of Eternity" motif carved above the arch of this beautifully imagined window in a tumbledown chapel in Donegal, Ireland.

that awakens perception of where you need to be next in your life.

"I suggest that people use a mythological point of view, to see everything on the journey on that frequency, not as a consumer. I provide them with a reading list, articles, maps, expectations of climate— want them to know what to expect, not be jarred by too much surprise. I tell them, *'Be prepared—then let go of expectations!'*"

On my journeys, I choose a theme. One of my favorite subjects is roads: cobbled streets, brick roads, dirt roads, old Roman paved roads—all manner of roads. Every time I photograph or sketch or write about them, I consider them for both their physical beauty and function and their allegorical meaning. I use the same practice for other deceptively simple things from everyday life, such as windows, doors, clouds, faces, children, café signs, bicycles, tilework, and bookstore facades. I've suggested the following exercise for the participants on my tours. For the first few days of our journey, we seek out one or two things that marshals the attention, seizes the imagination. Then for the rest of our travels together, I encourage them to try to focus on details: the doors of Dublin houses, Parisians with their dogs, roadside shrines in Turkey, tile patterns of Lisbon, the promenading rituals of Lisbon and Barcelona. We then take time to write, draw, photograph, and discuss what it is that attracts our attention, even our *love*. For there is no powerful pilgrimage without love, no memorable journey without the erotic, the presence of Eros animating, enlivening, vitalizing our walks, talks, visits, meals, and conversations.

In this way, we build our own memory theaters, or what California artist Maggie Oman calls "soul boxes." On her travels, she collects the oddments of each day: matchbooks, napkins, maps, ticket stubs, ripped-out pages of guidebooks, and her own sketches. Back home, she assembles them in boxes as a reminder of what touched her soul when she was on pilgrimage.

Art critic Robert Hughes reminds us that in the nineteenth century, "Every educated person drew as a matter of course.... Drawing was an ordinary form of speech, used as a pastime or *aide-memoire*, without pretensions to 'high' art. Nevertheless, this general graphic literacy was the compost form which the great depictive artists of the late nineteenth and early twentieth centuries were able to grow: Degas, Eakins, Picasso, Matisse. It was gradually abolished by the mass camera market."

As Lisa Dennis remarks in her book *The Traveler's Eye*, most tourists now, of course, "draw" with their cameras. The question of the day is: Does the average person see as well with the camera as with a pencil in the hand?

Hannah Hinchmann's book *A Trail Through Leaves* is an inspirational work to encourage the practice of rendering the world around you—either at home or on the road—by hand. The author's advice is to transcribe poetry by hand and write down places you will visit. She recommends a style of journal writing that includes smells, story-memories, and encounters with animals. "Write down your delirious sensory pitch," she suggests, and, most important, "cleave to verbs." Her antidote to boredom or the terror of lost time is to "do things that alter time." In much the same way as Whitman and Thoreau vaunt the benefits of daily walks, she teaches that before you can "capture the unmeasurable, first you must learn to notice it." Her most innovative exercise, and of utmost benefit for the pilgrim, is the daylong entry. In this, she encourages a rendering of a mosaic of impressions from words, drawings, and sound recordings—keeping the flavor of the day alive.

As artist Betty Edwards reminds us, "Drawing isn't the problem, *seeing* is the problem."

The problem of seeing *what?* The beauty made visible by seeing with the eyes of the heart.

Imagine the way you see yourself *seeing*. How are you seeing your way? How do you plan to record it, remember it, observe the journey as if it were a work of art? Try to see yourself as a peripatetic artist whose job it is to capture in words, art, music, or story the essential secret of the day. How would you do it? The practice you pursue will determine the quality of your pilgrimage.

Recall that in *Walden*, Thoreau describes his mornings as a "cheerful invitation to make my life of equal simplicity, and I may say, innocence, with Nature herself." His method of turning each day into a pilgrimage was rising early and bathing in the pond. He called it his religious exercise and a reflection of a story he knew about the characters inscribed on the bathing tub of King Tching-thang that read: "Renew thyself completely each day; do it again, and again, and forever again."

Joan Halifax is a Buddhist anthropologist and ecologist who has been a spiritual explorer all her life. In her book *A Fruitful Darkness* she writes about the miraculous discovery that "everybody has a geography itself that can be used for change. That is why we travel to far-off places. Whether we know it or not, we need to renew ourselves in territories that are fresh and wild. We need to come home through the body of alien lands. For some, these are journeys of change are taken intentionally and mindfully. They are pilgrimages, occasions when Earth heals us directly. Pilgrimage has been for me, and many others, a form of inquiry in action."

And you, fair traveler, how will you rejuvenate yourself each day?

THE ART OF WALKING

Solvitur ambulando. It is solved by walking.
—Saint Augustine

In his essay on the art of walking, Henry David Thoreau described his daily regimen of four-hour walks, a time when he could gather himself, hear the sound of his own heart beating—all while *sauntering*, as he was fond of calling it, a word, he wrote, "which ... is beautifully derived 'from idle people who roved about the country, in the Middle Ages, and asked charity, under pretense of going a la Sainte Terre,' to the Holy Land, till the children exclaimed, 'There goes a Sainte-Terre,' a Saunterer, a Holy-Lander."

Then remember the power of the traveler's lamp. With it, we can see the pages of an old Greek volume on mythology. Turning the pages, we read that one way to focus our drifting attention is to listen to the whisper of wind through treetops. The Greeks personified those dulcet tones as the movement of lovely dryads, wood nymphs, which is why poets are compelled to wander through the woods when they need to be inspired. In nature, on a walk in the woods, they knew they could take in the spirits, the gods and goddesses who linger on in the world.

An Alpine hiker, Bavaria, Germany.

Remember that contemplative walks transform the ground beneath us into holy ground, whether we're on the Appian Way outside Rome, or the parking lot outside our office building. The preparation for pilgrimage requires that we begin at home to watch and listen more attentively, despite being bombarded by everyday life.

Imagine how you might revive the art of walking on your journey. There are a multitude of reasons for doing so. First, it is a way to begin a modest training for the walking you will do on your journey; second, it is a way to begin to contemplate what your intentions and purposes are. But, as Thoreau himself said, *simplify*. Leave the cell phone at home. Take only pad and pencil with you. Walk where you can be alone with your thoughts. Allow the usual thoughts about work and errands to drift in and out again. Simply walk and be attentive to the surroundings of your neighborhood, the park, or shoreline. Consider a walking stick, the pilgrim's staff, for balance and constant contact with the earth.

In this spirit arises an image of gratitude and presence from Black Elk's story of the legend of White Buffalo Woman, who sang to her people:

> *In a sacred manner I am walking.*
> *With visible tracks I am walking.*
> *In a sacred manner I walk.*

In our own time, the Milwaukee poet Antler has written an homage to his walking staff.

STAFF

I have worn smooth with the grip of my hand
    branches found by the trail,
Caught by my eye and lifted,
Thrown in the air and caught by my hand and tested—
    if it's not too long,
    if it's not too short,
    if it feels just right,
I say to myself—"This is my staff!"
    and thump the ground with its end.

Carry me far! Take me where I must go!
Miles away from miles away from every road,
    every road, every human voice
    or voice of machine,
Through woods I love,
Past lakes where no one is,
Beyond where the footpath ends,
    up where the mountains glow
    and the sky has never been breathed! . . .

My walking stick urges me on,
    takes my hand like a friend,
Comforts me, steadies me
    over rough terrain,
Beyond where it's ever been mapped,
Where no human ever set foot,
Following the voice of the stream
    up where the mountains glow
    and the sky has never been breathed!

THE WAY OF FAITH

Hail, inexhaustible treasure of life!
—Akathist hymn to Mary

Religious historian Huston Smith finds four aspects to pilgrimage: singleness of purpose; freedom from distraction; ordeal or penance; and offerings. With relish, he tells of the "unexpected joy" he felt when he first encountered the traditional Jewish custom of offering alms. A friend at Duke University gave it to him, saying, "My commission to you is to give alms to the next Berkeley street person."

When I asked Smith why human beings have practiced sacred jour-neys as far back as we know, he deliberates, then says, "The fact is we are embodied souls; we have to act out our faith."

He admits with a certain bashfulness that when he has traveled with his wife, she chastens him for his exuberance about seeing the sacred sites. "Oh, not to set foot on them would be *wasting* such a valu-able opportunity. I have to see it for myself. My idea is to wake at dawn, then *Charge! Charge! Charge!*"

"Something else very peculiar about me," Smith adds disarmingly, "is my compulsion to take something back from sacred places. From every trip I have selected a stone that I have brought back to place in my garden here in Berkeley. I don't even know where they are from after all these years, but I feel their *power* around here somewhere!"

Finally, there is the internal aspect of pilgrimage, the counterpart to the exploration of the outer world. "That's what it's all about," Smith concludes. "Are we doing it out of rote or out of devotion?

My introduction to a living example of a life of devotion was through my own mother, Rosemary LaChance Cousineau. My child-hood is riddled with rhapsodies on a theme of faith. Today she is a florist in Sonoma, California, who vividly remembers the one bona fide pilgrimage she has been on. It was 1948 and she was sixteen years old when she accompanied her sister and brother-in-law on a car journey from Detroit to Quebec, where they visited the shrine of Saint Anne de Beaupré, in honor of the mother of the Blessed Mother. They saw at the shrine many lame and crippled pilgrims walking and prostrating themselves up the road and the half-completed staircase to the basilica. Inside were thousands of crutches and wheelchairs left behind by those cured through the years of faith-impelled visits. Besides the photos left behind by the cured, there was a panorama painted by local Canadians of the Stations of the Cross. It surrounded those who had crawled up the hill with a powerful association of art and healing and seemed to be its own reward for their acts of faith and endurance.

"It was the place to go in those years if you were desperate," my mother remembers, "where Americans and Canadians came for hope and miracles. My sister, Fran, was always tortured. I didn't know it then, but she was trying to find answers to her health problems and her demons, which turned out to be schizophrenia.

"I remember doing what I did on my own. I just wanted to," my mother continued. I believed in miracles and, looking back, I think I was doing it for my mom and dad and their health problems, for the expiation. Mom had a heart condition, and my dad always had a heart problem, but also what they called in those days a 'quiet drinking problem.'

"I came back to Detroit with a feeling of contentment. My parents didn't say anything direct to me—they always *masked* their feelings. But I sensed that they thought I came back a better person."

A few years later, my mother's sister took her son, who had been stricken with polio months before the vaccine appeared, to the shrine. He wasn't cured of the polio, but remarkably he did live and has thrived into middle age. She believes theirs was a case of prayers being answered "in a different, but powerful way."

Pilgrimage is "belief-in-action." My mother's faith was based on the lives of the mystics, and her underground network of support with her friends at the parish. Every Tuesday night, they went together to do their *novenas*, which allowed them to go *vicariously* on pilgrimage. Their priest was a Passionist, very fiery, who made you feel like you were right there, on the Via Dolorosa in Jerusalem. "Those miniature pilgrimages helped many a person through the Depression. Faith is all about what goes on between me and my Maker."

Mythology scholar Joan Marler was leading a tour through Ireland in the mid-1990s when she had to confront an inevitability for many travelers. After having jumped through hoops to get official permission to sail to the remote and usually storm-wracked Skellig Islands, she was elated to encounter magnificent weather. "All was horizon around us; the water was placid. We could truly feel the power of the ancient monks who had lived here alone for centuries, painstakingly copying out manuscripts." When the group returned to the mainland that night, however, there were problems with accommodations; several people became incensed and promptly forgot the epiphanies of the day.

"I tried to help them see how mundane our problems were compared with the extraordinary stroke of luck we had getting to the Skelligs *at all* that day, but, ironically, this mythically difficult journey proved to be too easy! So I learned that day that when travel is too easy, people often don't appreciate their experience and certainly don't understand the mythological nature of certain kinds of travel."

Imagine that the task of the pilgrim is to *deepen* the mystery for himself or herself, not have it handed over. If you find yourself facing disappointment, try to ask yourself where your attention has wandered. The real work on the journey has begun; you have to meet the gods at these ancient sites halfway.

Rejoice that you have come so far.

THE WAYS OF SOULFUL TRAVEL

Nothing comes from doing nothing
—William Shakespeare (1564–1616)

Through the years, I've received hundreds of phone calls, letters, messages, prods, and nudges to help others with their upcoming travels. I enjoy plying friends with reading lists, video and record lists, maps, guidebooks, and—best of all—stories that help demystify the road. I also suggest up front that travelers search guidebooks or the travel sections of their hometown papers for features on upcoming events in the countries that their pilgrimage will be taking them through.

Choosing appropriate celebrations, festivals, art, music, or literary exhibitions is a natural way to enrich your journey. The Hammer family from New York City, for example, attends lectures at their local museums and libraries to inspire their itineraries. A recent exhibit at the New York Library on the Romantic movement helped bring their journey through England's Lake District to life.

For one friend who had difficulty remembering details from his travels, I suggested he take on the task of writing a poem every day during his journey abroad. The daily task proved impossible for him, so he decided to focus his attention on a one-week stretch through Paris, Prague, and Florence. To this day, his memories of that time are the fondest of all his travels because, as he has told me, "when everything is a possible poem, the world is suddenly far more interesting."

ROAD RITUALS

Are you writing down the country?
—asked of René Caillié in Timbuktu

On the road to Santiago, pilgrims sang psalms and chants, some of which have come down to us. As Melczer noted, they were sung to strengthen the pilgrims' courage. I'm reminded of the tradition of singing among my own ancestral *voyageurs*, who canoed stupendous distances across Canada, singing in time to their paddle strokes. On their thirty-day pilgrimages to the sacred peyote fields, the Huichol

After an all-night ritual peyote meeting in the mountains of northern Mexico, a group of Huichol, Tarahumara, and Navajo Indians gather around their sacred altar and greet the rising sun with prayers and song.

Indians sing an elaborate round of songs to the maize gods, supplicating them that their harvest be a good one.

Music plays a major part in my own travels. For the past twenty years, one of my travel rituals has been to play a now much-battered cassette of Canned Heat's "On the Road Again" as I pack my bags. That freight-train harmonica at the beginning of the song and through the refrains never fails to put a smile on my face and humbleness in my heart as I'm reminded of my good fortune to be embarking once again.

For several of my early journeys, I recorded cassettes, streamlined and adapted for that particular trip: "Philippines Peregrinations, 1983"; "The Soul of Paris, 1996"; "Myth in the Mediterranean, 1993."

Playing the tapes on those journeys always stimulated my teaching and journal-writing; playing them afterward works in reverse, reminding me of the times and places of that journey.

Mort Rosenblum has an important ritual before going out on reporting assignments: He chooses a few tapes of his favorite music. Whether it's a human-interest story about the barges on the Seine, or the outbreak of war in Bosnia, he knows that his favorite tapes will help him keep perspective.

Because so much of what is encountered along the road is novel, it is important to honor it by recording our thoughts as we move along. Thinking that we'll remember the smell of the pine cones or the shimmering of the sea is as illusory as trying to convince ourselves that we'll perfectly recall a dream.

"When in doubt, write," an English teacher drummed into me long ago. Why is this so important? Because you are changing as the miles click off and the destination draws nearer, and there is nothing more fascinating than to closely observe the process of change and deepening, and how we respond to that quicksilver phenomenon. Bear in mind what the humble humorist James Thurber said when asked why he wrote: "I don't know what I think until I read what I have to say."

It's the *process* of writing a letter or in a journal that leads us to the truth of our evolving journey. Very often, the simpler and the slower, the better. I think of the sixteenth-century "Pilgrim of the Clouds," Yuan Hung-tao, who wrote brilliant travel essays and nature poetry during his keenly observed journeys to the sacred sites of China. It is his practice that thrills me the most. On his pilgrimage to Mount She, he writes:

> *I enter the temple, seek the dream world of*
> *the monks, thumb through the sutras,*
> *feel the dustiness of this traveler's life.*

In other poems, he describes getting up in the morning, saying good-bye to friends, or "Writing Down What I See," a simple, non-ego-based exercise that is like drawing with words.

If the dedication to the poetry of the ordinary is important, so is the very material of one's journal. My own belief is that it has to be leather for it to have soul. It must feel good as I lift it in my hands and lower it to a desk or café table. Leather also reminds me of the first books my grandfather and father gave me, and the rare books I've laid my hands on in old libraries. An array of writing tools is important for variety and for varying purposes—writing, drawing, painting, fooling around, playing.

The choice of guidebooks varies from journey to journey. I've taken the old standbys: Fodor's, Frommer's, Michelin, as well as the esoteric: *The Marvels of Rome*, a twelfth-century guide to the ruins of the city, and D. H. Lawrence's book on the Etruscans. These books have confirmed for me again and again the truth of what Paul Fussell alluded to when he said that great travel books are "Odes to Freedom ... and implicit celebrations of freedom in a world of prisons ... examples of personal freedom and philosophical courage ... like a poem, they give universal significance to local texture."

Other simple ways to make holy the travel day: candles for private moments, to bring soul into a soulless hotel room or to help your meditation on a loved one far away. The year my father died, I found my self in Périgueux, France, the town from which my ancestors came in 1678. I lit a votive candle for him and said a prayer for his soul's journey, an ancient ritual gesture designed to help the soul on its way through the darkness of infinity. Now not a trip goes by when I fail to light a candle for at least one friend or family member. Years ago, a dear friend was stricken with the reoccurrence of cancer she first had at age sixteen. In an inspired moment, I lit a candle I took for her in Chartres Cathedral on the day of her sixteen-hour operation. Two months later, she described to me how in the middle of the darkness, when things were "touch and

American expatriate Jeannette Hermann, on pilgrimage to Amiens Cathedral, France, and her young friend Jack Blue Cousineau, light a votive candle.

go" according to her doctors, she saw a flicker of candlelight.

For some travelers, carrying a nine-band radio would be foolhardy. But I grew up listening to a tiny palm-sized transistor radio with a metal clip attached to my windowsill. My radio could get ballgames all the way from California, which might have been the moon for all I knew. Today, I am still in awe of the magic of radios—the humbler, the better. To listen to the Voice of America, the BBC, or Radio Luxembourg from a remote place, as I've done from the Guatemala rainforest or deep in the Amazon, or even from a remote cottage on the west coast of Portugal, is to once again feel the raw nerves of the pilgrim. It *deepens* the mystery of traveling.

Another sacred aspect of travel is time. The practice of winding the old Timex I inherited from my father is one I look forward to each morning, especially when I am traveling. The diligence it demands makes me very aware of my continuity with him and with the winding of the days and years, and reminds me of the limited time there is for that particular journey.

THE WAY OF SERENDIPITY

Keeping to the main road is easy, but people
love to be sidetracked.
—Lao Tzu (6th century B.C.E.)

We can plan only so much. Then we must let go and trust in
Kairos, the old god of synchronicity. One of the masters of
this subtle move is architect Anthony Lawlor. With sheer glee, he tells
the story of how he became an "accidental pilgrim" to the *Field of
Dreams* baseball field outside Fairfield, Iowa.

"I didn't go intentionally," he said in a recent interview. "I was driving with my wife in rural Iowa, and near Dyersville, where they filmed
the movie, we saw a little homemade sign and immediately recognized
it and said, 'Hey, what the hell!' I'm glad we trusted our hunch, because
it was very low-key then. Just a few tourists tossing a ball around and
playing catch. It felt like a genuine connection with baseball in its
purest form. Pure play. I was thrown back to my childhood, the simple
beauty of the game, just for what it is."

Like many modern fans, Lawlor has grown wary of the commer-
cialization of baseball, a game that was once sacred to him. "Suddenly,
seeing this incredibly beautiful baseball field and remembering how
emotional the movie was took me back to when I was still enjoying the
game, even back to Little League memories."

He saw a simple sign explaining the history of the movie and says
that the setting, "the bright green field and white foul lines against the
dark red, nineteenth-century barn and farmhouse gave the scene a certain timelessness.

"For me it was a surprisingly authentic sacred site, really a dramatic
journey back to the source of the game, to the opening we all had as
kids. It was like accessing the source in more traditional forms of pilgrimage in places, like India, I've been to.

The oldest ballpark in America, Rickwood Field, founded in 1910, Birmingham, Alabama.

"Another ritual of mine is looking at maps. Just looking at where I'm at, how far I've progressed on my journey, reconnects me with my quest. If I'm aware of what I'm doing, it tells me where I am with my pilgrimage. Tells me how the pilgrimage has changed me. Just looking closely at the difference between old and new maps allows me to see how one layer of history lays over another, which can help me *imagine* the reality of a place like Paris, for instance.

"Recently, friends of mine went to India, and I created a little ceremony for them. I handed them a sacred bundle and simply said, 'Open it when you reach your goal.' Anyone can do this for their friends and family: a book, a candle, a pencil, a prayer written out by hand. They become sacred through your intention and the place they are opened."

Lawlor emphasizes soul in every aspect of his life and work. He points out that the relationship between leaving one's home every day and setting out on pilgrimage is similar.

"Stepping into the pilgrimage zone," as he puts it, "is like going into one's own unknown. It is a challenge to all who are still at home. The very existence of these sacred sites seems to ask of us, 'Are you alive now at home? Are you going to stay in your coffin of mediocrity, break out of your cage, and take a journey to discover this in order to find yourself?'"

Lawlor recommends finding a meaningful ritual to perform at key moments of the pilgrimage. "We need a ritual along the way—placing ashes along a river, flowers on a grave, or engaging in a ritual of that place—so we might truly feel the spirit of the place. So it's important to learn rituals ahead of time, such as going to a holy well at a certain time of the day."

As a supreme example of pilgrimage as a microcosm for life, Lawlor cites Borobudur, the magnificent Buddhist monument in Java, "a tour of the whole mythic journey in microcosm." Borobudur is an image of the sacred mountain; it holds sacred relics inside bell-shaped structures called *stupas*. On the walls of the ten terraces of the temple are scenes from the life of the Buddha and scenes depicting the journey of the pilgrim Sudhana.

A pilgrim en route to such a monument fasts, prays, and prepares for the ritual ascent which is understood as a kind of initiation. The circumambulation, walking clockwise around the temple, is meant to lift the pilgrim's consciousness to a higher plane. Unfortunately, Lawlor concludes, in our times the promise of true pilgrimage has been trivialized. "We've turned the ecstatic possibilities of pilgrimage into something tame like trips to Disneyland. We don't believe [or are in fear of] the ecstatic because of the Puritan streak in us. . . . What we're doing is creating predominantly an illusion of pilgrimage in pop culture, an illusion of *being there*. Virtual travel, entertainment."

Most of all, he says, we need to believe in the ecstatic again and

A panoramic view of the surrounding Kedu Plain from the upper terrace of Borobodur, an 1,100-year-old temple-mountain in Java, Indonesia.

know the difference between the illusion of the sacred and the real thing. Lawlor uses the Sanskrit term *tapas:* "It means giving up, sacrifice. The word *sacred* comes from *sacrifice*, to cut up. That means that in order to have a sacred journey, you have to give up something, sacrifice; but few people today in the West want to hear about that. Americans want the boon without the labyrinth.

"Pilgrimage starts the wheel," Lawlor concludes "It turns the wheel of *samsara*, the wheel of life, and we have to live with the consequences."

Imagine the burden on your back as your pilgrimage progresses. Besides the burden caused by overpacking, there are mental and spiritual burdens. Many times, the burden that a traveler carries is the heavy load of unasked questions. Here are a few that have helped me find my way in many a strange city and country: How was this city founded? What is the oldest building and street in town? Where can we find the best street market? Do you have any favorite places for music? Who is the patron saint? Where is the best place to watch the sunrise? Where can I find the most authentic music? Who is the most beloved poet here? Where can I find the best bookstore? Where can I go for a con-templative afternoon? Is there a promenade at dusk or dawn?

Try coming up with your equivalent of the traditional greeting of Tibetan travelers: "To which sublime tradition, revered sir, do you belong?"

Remember, those who don't ask essential questions don't find what's most authentic. The soul of your pilgrimage, the heart of your destination, disappears, will be invisible, like the Grail Castle if you are too afraid or too proud to appear as you really are at the moment—someone far, far from home, without all the answers, without the soul map to the city. Those who refuse to ask vital questions along the way pay the consequence, either by getting lost or by settling for the super-ficial gloss that is everywhere served up to the tourist on the fly. But there is another way. Besides not being bashful about asking locals about very practical matters such as the way to the nearest facilities, a pharmacy, the airport taxi, and the like, there is the way of the heart-opening questions. Reserve your most soulful questions for people who tend to be more receptive to travelers, such as café waiters and book-store owners.

Pilgrimage, like art and poetry, is at every station "concerned with meaning." The poet Muriel Rukeyser recalls a teacher asking her class, "How many of you know any other road in the city except the road between home and school?" She does not raise her hand. As a girl, she was already being shunned into silence, preventing her from answer-ing, ashamed of her response. "These are moments," she recalls years later, "at which one begins to see."

Imagine yourself at the crossroads. No one on an authentic pil-grimage will escape the moment. You have departed and you are on the road, brimming with exhilaration, anticipation, the thrill of movement. You have magnetized your journey with purpose. You will attract the things of the road like never before. But you will have to choose, daily. Meaning begins to cling to each encounter. Every day, you must choose which road sign to believe. Each day, whether you are walking 2,000 miles from Denmark to Santiago, driving to Graceland, or taking a bus to Chekhov's home in Yalta, you will have to choose— between the *image* that is being offered to the great run of people alongside you, or the *imaginative*, active encounter with the place. Do not be fooled by *glamour*, an old Scottish word for spell. The glamour of Versailles can entrance you, but hypnosis can deaden your eyes.

The question at the heart of the quest is how to renew our power of vision.

THE NECESSITY OF RUINS

Man is a god in ruins.
—Emerson

The wandering French essayist Jacques Réda reminds himself before he leaves his Paris apartment every Sunday morning for his long strolls around the city to see *one new thing*. This is quite a challenge, but as someone dedicated to seeing something new in the old he has learned to notice what others ignore.

To see this way is to move closer to the secret heart of the world. It is an indirect movement, represented throughout the world as a spiral, the symbol of the life-force itself at the crossroads of time and space.

The practice of soulful travel is to discover the overlapping point between history and everyday life, the way to find the essence of every place, every day: in the markets, small chapels, out-of-the-way parks, craft shops. Curiosity about the extraordinary in the ordinary moves the heart of the traveler intent on seeing behind the veil of tourism.

In other words, as the Bronx oracle Yogi Berra said, "If you come to a fork in the road—take it!"

THE ODDYSSEYS

Don't get even, get odd!
—A. Nonymous, Zen master

Then there are the offbeat pilgrimages as "oddysseys," the curiousity cabinet of world travel lore. Today that cabinet would be full to bursting. Inside would be advertisements for "pilgrimages" to the exhibits in Dallas' Sixth-Floor Museum, illustrating one of the most tragic dates in American history, November 22, 1963. Visitors can look out the same window of the Texas School Book Depository building from which Lee Harvey Oswald aimed his rifle and fired the shots that changed the country forever. In Phnom Penh, the present government has turned the Tuol Sleng high school that was used by the Khmer Rouge for torture chambers into a museum so that foreign visitors might better understand the magnitude of Pol Pot's inferno. Old K.G.B. offices in St. Petersburg, Russia, and Vilnius, Lithuania, have also been whitewashed and now hang the shingle of tourism in an attempt to lure tourist dollars. It may give a traveler the "gruesomes," as D. H. Lawrence called them, until you remember that for centuries pilgrims purred with delight at the opportunity to "pay homage" to the skulls and femur bones piled high in the catacombs beneath Rome and Paris.

Along other new pilgrimage routes, we find the former studio of Georgia O'Keefe in Abiquiu, New Mexico, the first museum in America to be devoted to a female artist of world stature. Art pilgrims are venturing there to bask in the desert light of her art. Covered bridges in Madison County, Iowa, now attract movie buffs who want to see where the Clint Eastwood/Meryl Streep movie was filmed; and in

Graveyard and cathedral in St. David's, Wales, on All Soul's Day, a particularly good day to visit an ancestral resting place.

San Francisco, Grey Bus Line tours drive by the *Mrs. Doubtfire* house in which Robin Williams' lovable cross-dressing character lived. Other eccentric but perfectly legitimate recent pilgrimages I've seen advertised in the *New York Times* are "Pilgrimages to Graffiti Sites," designed for European graffiti artists who long to go to the sacred source of anarchist street art.

Never a place to let a tour go undone, one of the most outrageous modern pilgrimages takes place every day in Hollywood, California. In a gleaming black hearse driven by a tour guide dressed as an undertaker, the intrepid pilgrim can visit the gravesites, overdose havens, and various places of demise of the rich, famous, and dead. In Woodlawn Cemetery in the Bronx, New York, thousands go to hear music concerts near the gravesites of Duke Ellington, Miles Davis, and George M. Cohan. Pilgrimages to Highgate Cemetery in London and Montparnasse Cemetery in Paris are common, as are trips to make gravestone rubbings or collect epitaphs. Some pilgrims can get carried away, however. In December 1997, the *Wall Street Journal* reported a story about Mar Walters of Augusta, Georgia, who has been research-ing graveyards from Atlanta to Iona, Scotland. One time he was so pre-occupied studying a tombstone in rural Illinois that he fell into an open grave. "We were laughing so hard I could hardly crawl out," he said later.

Not to worry. The god of pilgrimage wears many masks. There is a grace and dignity to all who seek. Landscape scholar and immortal-izer of road culture in America J. B. Jackson says in *The Necessity for Ruins*, "The inspiration of tourism is a desire to know more about our-selves. If we offend public taste, that is only incidental to our search; the Swiss cuckoo clock, the bumper sticker from Carlsbad Caverns is a type of diploma—proof that we have at least *tried* to improve our-selves."

Improve ourselves *how?* you might wonder. Perhaps by constantly working the imagination, seeking metaphors for the human condition, gazing into as many mirrors and walking down as many roads as possible.

THE SECRET OF SOULFUL TRAVEL

The beauty of the Way is that there is no "way."
—Loy Ching-Yuen, *The Book of the Heart*

The secret, of course, is that there is no secret. No one way, just *your* way.
How else can I tell you this?

In 1819, a blind soldier, James Holman, was invalided out of the British Navy. He promptly set out to see the world. He traveled alone, except for one brief stint with a deaf man. He spoke none of the languages he encountered, and moved about by public transit. Upon return, he published several travel books in which he wrote that he rarely felt he missed anything because of his blindness. Noticing his condition, people were always inviting him to "squeeze things" as a way of perceiving them.

"And this is what the contemporary travel writer may have to do," wrote Anatole Broyard in his essay on Holman. "He may have to *squeeze* places until they yield something, anything."

"Squeeze the feeling," as Van Morrison moans. Touch the place or risk not being touched, touch the world with the hands of the wandering traveler. Squeeze places as deliberately as photographer Jim Brandenburg, who spent ninety days in the northern woods of Minnesota, shooting only one image a day. Squeeze them gently, as that indefatigable traveler Rose Macaulay reflected on the ruins of Athens, "This broken beauty is all we have of that ancient magnificence; we cherish it like the extant fragments of some lost and noble poem."

"I'm a soul in wonder ... I'm a soul in wonder ... I'm a soul in wonder," Van Morrison chants. It's the finest description of the pilgrim I know.

What does any of this mean for a traveler seeking the unknown place of renewal? Just this: There is in pilgrimage, as there is in architecture and psychology and poetry, *a secret room*. Donald Hall tells of friends who bought an old farmhouse in the countryside. It was a "warren of small rooms," and once they settled in and began to furnish their new home they realized that the lay of the house made little sense. "Peeling off some wallpaper, they found a door that they pried open to reveal a tiny room, sealed off and hidden, goodness knows why: They found no corpses nor stolen goods." For Hall, the mystery of poetry to evoke powerful feelings finds its analogy here, in its ability to be sealed away from explanation, this is the place where "the unsayable gathers."

And so it is on the pilgrim's path. Everywhere you go, there is a secret room. To discover it, you must knock on walls, as the detective does in mystery houses, and listen for the echo that portends the secret passage. You must pull books off shelves to see if the library shelf swings open to reveal the hidden room.

I'll say this again: Everywhere has a secret room. You must find your own, in a small chapel, a tiny café, a quiet park, the home of a new friend, the pew where the morning light strikes the rose window just so.

As a pilgrim you must find it or you will never understand the hidden reasons why you really left home.

Pilgrim, pass by that which you cannot love.

The Five Excellent Practices
of Pilgrimages

Inspired by a fifth-century conversation between Zi Zhang and Confucius about the practices of wise rulers in *The Analects*, here are five excellent practices for travelers on sacred journeys:

> *Practice the arts of attention and listening.*
> *Practice renewing yourself every day.*
> *Practice meandering toward the center of every place.*
> *Practice the ritual of reading sacred texts.*
> *Practice gratitude and praise-singing.*

V

THE LABYRINTH

Furthermore, we have not even to risk the
adventure alone, for the heroes of all time have
gone before us. The labyrinth is thoroughly known.
We have only to follow the thread of the hero path,
and where we had thought to find an abomination,
we shall find a god. And where we had thought to
slay another, we shall slay ourselves. Where we had
thought to travel outward, we will come to the
center of our own existence. And where we had
thought to be alone, we will be with all the world.

—Joseph Campbell

WE KNOW ALL TOO WELL THAT FEW JOURNEYS ARE LINEAR and predictable. Instead they swerve and turn, twist and double back, until we don't know if we're coming or going. The image of the labyrinth is an ancient symbol for the meandering path of the soul that goes from light into darkness and emerges once again into light. With our backs against the wall of the labyrinth and the shouts of the beast sending shivers through our souls, we look around for a clue, any clue, to help us escape.

Curiously enough, our word *clue* comes from the old word *clew*, the name given to the gold thread that Ariadne gave to Theseus so he might find his way through—and back—from the heart of the labyrinth. That thin string we follow into the darkness—our intuition, our hunches, our dreams—is our *clew*.

"There is an island called Crete in the midst of the wine-dark sea," writes Homer, "a fair land and rich, begirt with water, and therein are many men innumerable, and ninety cities.... And among these cities is the mighty city of Knossus, wherein Minos when he was nine years old began to rule, he who held converse with great Zeus...."

During the halcyon days, ancient Crete was a peaceful kingdom. One day a strange child, half-man, half-bull, was born to Queen Pasiphaë. The cuckolded king was stricken with shame. Minos commissioned Daedalus, the most famous inventor in the kingdom, to design a prison for his son. Daedalus was renowned for his ingenuity, having invented blacksmithing, carpentry, armory, the chariot, and wax wings for his son Icarus. But even he was daunted by the task of hiding a beast whose cries could be heard from one end of the island to the other.

Then Daedalus chanced upon the young princess, Ariadne, as she was performing the Dance of Cranes. Her footsteps wove a pattern of graceful spirals. At once the inventor saw in the sand beneath the feet of the princess the outlines for a high-walled, seven-circuit labyrinth that would be built in the heart of the many-roomed palace. There, Minos concealed the howling beast.

But now, the king had two more problems: how to staunch the appetite of his insatiable monster, and how to keep Athens, his rival power, hostage to his reign of control over the Mediterranean. Minos' solution to ensure peace between the kingdoms was a deadly tribute. Seven maidens and seven boys were to be sent by ship every year from Athens as sacrifices to the Minotaur.

At last, the Greek prince Theseus could stand the humiliation no longer. He convinced his father, Aegeus, to let him be one of the seven youths. When Theseus arrived on the shores of the distant island, he was seen by Ariadne, who was inflamed with passion for him. She pleaded with Daedalus to help her in saving Theseus' life so she might have him for her own, and earn passage from her father's island kingdom.

Flattered by the princess' request, Daedalus surrendered the secret to his labyrinth. "Take this enchanted ball of thread with you tonight," he counseled. "When the parade of youths pass by, slip the ball into the hands of the young prince Theseus. Whisper to him as he passes underneath the lintel of the entrance to the labyrinth that he must quickly fasten one end of it, then let the ball unroll until he reaches the center."

This the prince did. Through the shadow-strewn passages he walked, unafraid because of the power of destiny he felt in his hand as he unrolled the *clew*, the ball of thread. Stepping over the bodies of the mangled youths, he followed the sound of the Minotaur's groans.

What happened next is lost in the annals of history and mythology. Some say Theseus thrust a sword into the beast's heart; others say that he quickly strangled it.

After the deed was done, Theseus followed the *clew*, turn by tortu-ous turn, back to the entrance of the labyrinth, rolling it back into a ball to return to his Ariadne. She accepted his hand and they dashed together to the waiting boats in the harbor. Quickly, they sailed away to the nearby island of Naxos, where Theseus left behind his savior out of fear that she might be in danger back in the ever-resentful courts of Athens. As the fates would have it, only moments after waking alone on the sands of Naxos, and watching in terror as her lover's ship dis-appeared out to sea, the god Dionysus magically appeared to Ariadne. The great weavers spun on into the night, weaving a different destiny for her.

The telltale sign of a mythic story or image is its inexhaustible nature. So it is with the myth of the labyrinth, at once a poignant psy-chological story and an allegory for the shift of power between the Greeks and Minoans in ancient times. In Jorge Luis Borges' short story *The House of Asterion*, the plot twists are seen from the lonely point of view of the Minotaur.

"The morning sun reverberated from the bronze sword," the story ends. "There was no longer even a vestige of blood."

"Would you believe it, Ariadne?" said Theseus. "The Minotaur scarcely defended himself."

The poet follows the clues of ancient writers who suggest that the Minotaur, weary of his imprisonment, of the killing, and of the shame his mother felt for him, was glad to see Theseus and calmly accepted his fate.

Mircea Eliade used this story to describe the central metaphor of his life's work. "A labyrinth is a defense," he said in his book *Ordeal by Labyrinth*, "sometimes a magical defense, built to guard a center, a treasure, a meaning. Entering it can be a rite of initiation, as we see in the Theseus myth. That symbolism is the model of all existence, which passes through many ordeals in order to journey toward its own cen-ter, toward itself, toward *atman*, as the Hindus call it." Eliade believed that the story represented the agony of temporarily losing hope. "There have been occasions," he said in an interview, "when I have been aware of emerging from a labyrinth, or of coming across a thread.... Of course, I didn't actually say to myself, 'I am lost in the labyrinth.' And yet, in the end, I did very much have the feeling of hav-ing emerged from a labyrinth as a victor. Everyone has had that expe-rience. But one must also add that there is not just *one* labyrinth. The trial, the ordeal, recurs again and again, throughout life. That is the ordeal. That is the hope for renewal. Each passage stretches and releases us."

Imagine your journey as labyrinthine. One of the central gifts of myth is that within each story they show us the full 360-degree circle of human behavior; we get to see for ourselves which arc of behavior we are currently acting out. Where are you now on the arc of that story? With whom do you identify? The inventor? The princess? The prince? The banished Minotaur? What is it like living out the myth of inventiveness, passionate love, heroic adventure, exile, and sacrifice?

For the pilgrim traveling a great distance and at great personal expense, the image of a path coiling into a labyrinth as the destination nears is a powerful one. Fear, sacrifice, confusion, betrayal, theft, even death are the invariables travelers are loathe to think about. The sheer physical exertion of the thousand-mile walk to a saint's tomb can evoke strong emotions of resentment and doubt; the loss of money, passport, or a travel companion can threaten a long-planned journey. You may have been given wrong directions, or perhaps were deliberately entrapped by con artists. Your baggage may have been misdirected and not returned to you for a week. You may feel savaged with disappoint-ments about the people with whom you are fated to travel on a group pilgrimage. Unaccustomed loneliness, unfamiliar food, unexpectedly kitschy architecture at the shrine you have dreamed of visiting all your life—all these disappoints can result in the confusion, frustration, and chaos that have been symbolized for centuries in the image of the labyrinth.

And yet, as Aldous Huxley has written, "Experience is not what happens to you, it is what you *do* with what happens to you."

Ask yourself what form your *clew* will be as the inevitable darkness and dismay descend on your journey. Patience, silence, trust, and faith are venerable qualities of the pilgrim, but more important is the *practice* of them.

No one ever escaped the shadowy corridors of a labyrinth without them.

THE TORTUOUS PATH

Three times in a year shall all thy males appear before the Lord thy God
in the place which he shall choose: in the feast of unleavened bread,
and in the feast of weeks and in the feast of tabernacles.
—Deuteronomy XVI: 16

Gary Rhine is a Jewish filmmaker and student of Hasidism whose lifelong dream had been to make a pilgrimage to Israel. Finally, in 1990, he ventured there with his youngest daughter, Odessa. Although much of the visit was soul-stirring, he also experienced a ter-rifying sadness.

> One of the highlights, or maybe I should call it a low point of the
> trip, was our visit to Yad Vashem, the Holocaust museum in
> Jerusalem. We spent several hours experiencing the multimedia

presentations describing the horrible events which befell the European Jews. We saw the museum collection of uniforms and weapons of the perpetrators, and the personal possessions of the victims, and letters and poetry they wrote and paintings they created during that time.

We spent the last part of the day in a unique memorial to the children killed by the Nazis. Standing in a darkened room, lit only by the stars of a synthetically created night sky, we listened to the names, one by one, of the young victims. The names went on and on and on. As I stood there crying, I felt the energy from my heart and from my soul draining out.

For the next many days, I felt spiritually empty. Questions gnawed. How could human beings get themselves to a state of mind to want to do these terrible things to other humans? How could the rest of the world have allowed it to happen? And the most daunting question for me—if humanity is capable of such evil toward one another, what's the use of working to make the world a better place? Because up until then, I believed it was my responsibility as a spiritual person to make serious efforts to improve the state of the world. But why? What could I do that would ever overcome this amazing potential for evil?

During the flight home, as my daughter slept, I had a realization. The appropriate reaction to this experience was not one of giving up. It was to double my efforts. If humanity was capable of astounding evil, then it must also be capable of astounding goodness and compassion. I needed to do something strong to offset the evil. Immediately, I felt myself filling back up with energy. In only a couple minutes, I went from the empty, wilted, and *depressed feeling I'd carried around since Yad Vashem to an abundant, crisp, and determined feeling. My next realization was that what had just happened to me was a religious experience, an epiphany. My pilgrimage initiated my life's work.*

Rhine's use of the word *initiated* is a soulful reflection of Eliade's belief that the purpose of the labyrinthine journey is exactly an initiation to a higher plane of consciousness. Reaching the center reorients us through a revelation of the sacred, however disturbing. "For me," Eliade writes, "the sacred is always the revelation of the real, an encounter with that which saves us by giving us meaning to our existence." Disturbing as it was to see into the horror of the labyrinth, the heart of darkness, it was also illuminating. This is the religious aspect of the dark stretch of the pilgrimage. *Religion* originally meant "to bind back," in the sense of reconnecting to a fundamental reality. "Religion for me," reflects Huston Smith, "is the search for the Real, and the effort to approximate one's life to it."

For the pilgrim, the traveler with a deep purpose, this is the moment of truth, when the search for the *real* takes you to a place that pierces your heart.

I still recall with a growling of grief deep in my heart an encounter with the face of evil. I had ventured into southern Germany in the fall of 1974 to celebrate Oktoberfest in Munich, which I did for nine straight days. On the tenth day, I broke away. I needed to face the sinister side of recent history and so I took a train to nearby Dachau. As I walked through the concentration camp, all my notions about knowing what had happened during the war through books and the stories of my war hero uncles were shattered. Standing before the metal gates to the Nazi torture chambers and ovens was a searing rite of passage. I felt irrevocably cut off from any last threads of innocence. Yet, as I looked around at the other tormented visitors that day, I was convinced of the healing power of pilgrimage to history's infernos. We need to see the monster hidden in the dark recesses of the world's labyrinthine history; we must remind ourselves there are *clews* to help us find our way back out again.

THE SHADOWSIDE

To know something, then, we must be scrubbed raw,
the fasting heart exposed.
—Gretel Ehrlich

For travelers, the element of shadow and danger is very real. Since the earliest caravans rolled over the sands of Asia, travel has been slow and precarious. Roads have traditionally been haunted by scoundrels. Despite their holy aura, pilgrims have never been exempt from the dangers of the open road. The shadow stalking the history of pilgrimage, like the Minotaur licking his chops in the tortuous passages of the king's labyrinth, is illustrated in the following passage,

A San Francisco graffiti artist makes a social critique with which anyone "lost" in the labyrinth of their journey can identify.

written in 1280, by the Pilgrim of Burchard:

> *Whenever someone was a malefactor such as a murderer, a rob-*
> *ber, a thief, or an adulterer, he used to cross the sea, either as a*
> *penitent, or else because he feared for his skin and therefore did*
> *not dare to stay in his own country; and so they came thither*
> *from all parts, such as Germany, Italy, France, England, Spain,*
> *Hungary, and other parts of the world. And while they change*
> *the sky above them they do not change their minds. Once being*
> *here, after they have spent what they had brought with them, they*
> *have to acquire new [funds] and so, they return to their "vomit,"*
> *doing the worse of the worst. . . .*

Nineteenth-century adventurer Isabella Bird gallivanted around the world and wrote about it brilliantly at a time when Victorian society considered it highly improper for a well-bred woman to be seen alone in public, much less support herself off the talent of her energy and her genius. Her explorations took her to Tibet, Hawaii, Japan, China, Korea, and through the Rocky Mountains. She was eternally optimistic on her expeditions, but there was one journey that gravely disappointed her—a pilgrimage on camelback to Mount Sinai. Her biographer describes this trip as a personal mission: Isabella had vowed to see the spot where Moses received the Ten Commandments. The journey was monotonous and exhausting, however. The team ran out of water, and she arrived at the Chapel of the Burning Bush at Saint Catherine's monastery overcome with fatigue and emotion.

She met with a rude welcome. The monks tried to extort money from her, exhorted her to buy worthless souvenirs, and appeared drunk from the wine they made at their own distillery. "I almost wish I had abstained from visiting," she wrote later. "How much of hollow mockery there is in its gorgeous church, its silver cymbals, its library of precious manuscripts, its ceaseless services!"

Gravely disappointed but still determined, she woke early the next morning and rode out to Gebel Musa with a guide, where she drank from the Fountain of Moses, the legendary spring that erupted where Moses kept his flocks of sheep. She then rode to the top of the 7,000-foot summit and looked down over the magnificent desert.

"For many years, from early childhood upwards," she wrote, "have I thought and dreamed about this mountain top, and I have imagined its aspect! ... It was worth all the desert heat and dreariness, the raging thirst, the relentless hot wind, and burning glare. It is the grandest mountain view I have ever seen. Completely silent, unutterably lonely, awfully silent."

Jo Beaton was a student at Syracuse University in upstate New York when she became committed to the antinuclear movement. She has made many significant journeys to some of the world's most powerful sacred sites, but in retrospect she believes that one stands out as a "deeply soul-searing pilgrimage."

> As a student in London in 1985, I was lucky enough to visit
> the women's peace camp at Greenham Common. I'd been deeply
> moved by the stories I'd heard about the thousands of women
> who had demonstrated at that RAF base against the placement
> of U.S. cruise missiles; women who were desperate and furious
> about the escalating arms race and the fact that the presence of
> nuclear warheads made Britain more of a target than ever. I
> was humbled yet enraged to learn that my own country was
> working to stockpile enough weapons there with the strength to
> destroy more than 1,500 cities the size of Hiroshima. Women
> had continually camped, protested, and taken direct action there
> for four years by the time I made my pilgrimage that October.
> The impact of meeting those fabulous and diverse women who

dedicated their lives towards such an enormous goal is still strong within me. Sleeping in their makeshift tents, sharing their modest fare, talking with them and witnessing firsthand their powerful dedication towards ending the nuclear arms race is an experience that guides me to this day. I'd been an active feminist since my teenage years, and earned a minor in women's studies in college, but the Greenham Common pilgrimage opened me up to the then newly forming ideas of ecofeminism and the environmental movement. Upon moving west, I joined a local Greens group, which had been inspired by the successful Green Party in Germany. In addition to working towards making the Greens a viable political party and getting on the California state ballot, we labored to get a local Nuclear Free Zone initiative passed—a grueling effort I was inspired to commit to as a result of another inspiring pilgrimage.

With my Greens affinity group (we called ourselves the Cockroaches), I journeyed through the seemingly endless dust-choked desert to reach the Nevada Test Site peace encampment. The camp there was dedicated to ending all nuclear weapons testing by heightening the general public's awareness of the dire need for a Comprehensive Test Ban. My experiences there of planning and taking direct action in solidarity with my group; getting arrested; participating in the spiral dance and other women's rituals in the holding areas; meeting the other test site pilgrims who had gathered from all over the earth; and through honoring the Shoshone land that our government has horrifically desecrated, were all potent and unforgettable. I keep those memories and draw from that strength and solidarity whenever I feel a lack of the same.

Pilgrims to the women's peace camp at Greenham Common tied bright ribbons of remembrance, doves of peace, and other ritual offerings onto the chain-link fence surrounding the military base in England.

Since Perestroika, the crumbling of the Berlin Wall, the end to our underground testing, and the ensuing changes that are still being made in international nuclear arms treaties, I believe that those millions of peaceful pilgrims have been enormously success-ful. Their efforts to alter the course of history, to turn the sites of very real evil into monuments of peace and change make them, to me, truly holy.

THE RELUCTANT PILGRIM

A journey is a fragment of hell.

—Mohammed

B ob Cooper is a retired real estate salesman from northern California. With deep sadness, he describes how his arrival in one of the German cities that he bombed as a World War II pilot was transformed into a powerful pilgrimage:

> *I flew thirty-five missions over Germany, dropping tons of high explosive. With sophisticated equipment, we felt our bombs usually hit close to our military objectives. But reason told me then, and tells me now, that we must have missed often enough—and in the process perhaps killed civilians, including, probably, mothers and children.*

> *In 1969, twenty-five years after I dropped my final bomb, I visited Germany via the Eurail system, spending about a week at various towns and cities, many of which I remembered as having bombed. As we stopped at each place for an overnight, I wondered if some of the older people there had been residents during the time I was bombing in 1945 and, if so, what their thoughts would be if they knew a former bomber pilot was enjoying their hospitality now.*

> *One night in Mainz, a beautiful city on the Rhine River, while my wife guarded our luggage in the railway station, I scouted for a pension for the night. I found one I liked, right on the river, and was taken upstairs where three older Germans, two men and a woman, made arrangements for the overnight stop. I spoke no German; they spoke no English. Even so, we had no difficulty in arriving at a fair price for the room. As I stood in that typically*

German room, I suddenly remembered that I had bombed a rail-
way bridge at the edge of the city. (Later, I identified the mission
as my sixth, on January 13, 1945.) The bridge was close to
town, and at least thirty-five bombers had unloaded bombs on
that target. How many had missed and hit the adjoining city?
I wondered. It gave me an eerie feeling to realize that I might be
talking now with Germans who had suffered grievous losses from
that strike so many years ago. If I had spoken their language,
I might have brought up the subject, albeit with trepidation. And
I might have apologized. As it was, I left that room with ques-
tions still unanswered, and wonder and a deep sadness.

Only in later years has Bob Cooper realized how that chance night in one of the cities he bombed gave him an opportunity to work through some of his own grief. The repeated telling of the story to friends through the years was a way of working through the unre-solved pain and the irony of vacationing in a place he had once helped destroy, even if in what he firmly believed was a just cause.

When Cooper's friend Art Eichhorn retired in the spring of 1988, he wanted to have some quality time to himself. He decided to make a cross-country pilgrimage in his Ford pickup truck and Apache tent trailer. He wanted to see his country at his own pace, after thirty long years of government employment.

One of the most lasting and emotional experiences I had on this
trip occurred when I was spent a week in Washington, D.C. I
made the pilgrimage to the Vietnam War Memorial. When I
arrived at the shrine, I got down on my knees in front of it in an
attempt to adjust the tripod of my camera, set with a wide-angle
lens in hopes of capturing an interesting scene which included
some tired flowers left behind by some vets, and a unique

upwards and elongated view of the wall. As I looked into my
viewfinder, I realized that an elderly couple had moved into my
picture. I watched as the man held a small piece of tissue against
the wall while the woman rubbed it very carefully with a pencil.
They looked at the name that had been transferred onto the tissue,
embraced each other tightly and quietly cried together. I never
heard a word spoken in these few short moments, but realized
that I had just experienced a tender act of love that vividly
remains in my memory to this day.

This story reflects one of the oldest strands of tradition in pilgrim-age: the graveside visit, the paying of homage to a loved one or someone you admired. Every time I return to the Detroit area, I make a point of going to the grave of my father. I take some flowers, pull the weeds around the gravestone, say a few prayers, and talk to him about our life together. It is a bittersweet experience, but one I would never miss.

In the late 1980s, I was standing next to rock star Jim Morrison's grave in Père-Lachaise cemetery in Paris with a group I was leading on a tour. Having worked for five years on a book with John Densmore, the Doors' drummer, I was brimming with stories about those turbu-lent times. Afterward, a swarthy young man approached me. "You worked with the Doors?" he asked me incredulously, barely able to speak. "I am from East Germany. I have been here to Morrison's grave thirty-three times now." He paused and looked back at the rainbow of colors painted onto Morrison's bust atop the grave. "The first time I came I *walked*."

"Why, why have you come so far?" I asked him with astonishment.

"He understood."

"Understood what?" I asked.

"How to *Break on Through*," he answered, under his breath, "How to get to the other side." Then he faded away into the crowd gathered around the poet's tombstone.

The graffiti-emblazoned, flower-bedecked gravesite of Jim Morrison in Paris, France.

FOR WANT OF SURPRISES

An inch of surprise leads to a mile of gratefulness.
—Brother David Steindl-Rast

With a slight but significant shift of perspective required of a pilgrim on a sacred journey, what was once a snarl becomes a test, disappointment turns into challenge. Nineteenth-century

French poet Théophile Gautier illustrates this in his storied travels through Andalusia, recounted in *Wanderings in Spain:*

> *Traveling becomes a reality, an action in which you take a part. In a diligence [coach] a man is no longer a man, he is but an inert object, a bale of goods, does not much differ from a portman-teau. He is thrown from one place to the other, and might as well stop at home. The pleasure of traveling consists in the obstacles, the fatigue, and even the danger. What charm can any one find in an excursion, when he is always sure of reaching his destina-tion, of having horses ready waiting for him, a soft bed, an excel-lent supper, and all the ease and comfort which he can enjoy in his own home! One of the great misfortunes of modern life is the want of any sudden surprise, and the absence of all adventures. Everything is so well arranged, so admirably combined, so plainly labeled, that chance is an utter impossibility; if we go on progress-ing, in this fashion, towards perfection for another century, every man will be able to foresee everything that will happen to him from the day of his birth to the day of his death. Humanity will be completely annihilated. There will be no more crimes, no more virtues, no more characters, no more originality. It will be impos-sible to distinguish a Russian from a Spaniard, an Englishman from a Chinese, or a Frenchman from an American. People will not even be able to recognize one another, for every one will be alike. An intense feeling of ennui will then take possession of the universe. . . .*

What is remarkable about this passage is Gautier's foresight into the plight of too many modern travelers: the washing out of cultural differences among nationalities, the overarching ennui of trendy cyni-cism, the lack of pleasure in a journey with no surprises. His remarks are a model for those trying to find a way to allow for synchronicity in their travels.

Granted, there comes a time for many a traveler when the bloom is off the rose. There is a hankering for home, and dread of one more day of "famous" sites with the group. But, as Freya Stark wrote in her book on Alexander the Great, "A good traveler does not, I think, much mind the uninteresting places. He is there to be inside them, as a thread is inside the necklace it strings. The world, with unknown and unexpected variety, is a part of his own Leisure; and this living participation is, I think, what separates the traveler and the tourist, who remains separate, as if he were at a theatre, and not himself a part of whatever the show may be."

Imagine the moment when you "hit the wall" on your journey. You're tired, you've lost track of your original purpose for taking the pilgrimage. Your feet hurt, your eyes smart, you are feeling angry with other travelers in your group or toward the local people you are encountering. What to do?

Try taking a day to *brood*. Take your good old time, by yourself, and sit on it. Time and patience are the most natural therapists in the world. Chances are that the frustration you are feeling comes from what you're missing more than from what you're seeing.

Think of the darkness as potentially *healing*. It may even be the appearance of what Spanish poet Frederico García Lorca called *duende*—the "dark sounds" in music, dancing, poetry, the ritual of the bullfight, the roots of all art. Goethe described *duende* as "a mysterious power that everyone feels but that no philosopher has explained." It is the "dark and quivering" companion to the muse and the angel, the other two sources of inspiration and mysterious gift-giving to human beings. "The real struggle is with the *duende*," Lorca writes. To find it there needs "neither map nor discipline." It appears. As a voice of shadow, as fury and fire.

For Lorca, the dark sounds portend the tenderness that emerges after a brush with mortality. It is deeper than the melancholy of the muse, the wistfulness of angels. "The *duende*—where is the *duende?*" he asks. "Through the empty arch comes an air of the mind that blows insistently over the heads of the dead, in search of new landscapes and unsuspected accents; an air smelling of a child's saliva, of pounded grass, and medusal veil announcing the constant baptism of newly created things."

THE DRAGONS OF DISAPPOINTMENT

Things are always different from what they might be.
—Henry James

With considerable chagrin about his disappointing experience at the palace of Knossus on Crete, archaeology scholar Michael Guillén recalls, "I felt very little at the site itself because of all the crowds and the meddling that had been done with the restoration; the only real power I felt was in the surrounding land. I felt that the site had been transmogrified, and that the only spirits left were in the objects in the museum. I suppose this is the danger of mass pilgrimage, the loss of spirit at the site, especially when the gods flee to higher and higher places."

The question, he agrees, as always, is what your attitude is toward these awkward moments, these radically disappointing moments in life.

"You have to steal what I call 'Intimate Moments' from the public. I learned that at the Maya site of Yaxchilan in Mexico. We were told

The steep walls of the Temple of the Great Jaguar (Temple I), seen from within the labyrinthine passages of Temple II, Tikal, Guatemala.

not to be at the site at night, and I repeated that to everyone in my tour one year. But after they had all fallen asleep, I snuck in with my co-leader, Sharon Matola [head of the Belize Zoo], because I knew she was a kindred spirit. It turned out to be my favorite moment of that tour, because I knew I had earned it. You see, you have to want to learn, to engage the spirits of the site, one on one.

"Living with the HIV virus, I don't feel as comfortable going to remote places anymore, so I have to go inside, inner pilgrimage to memory of old times. I'm stealing moments to learn the importance of time and memory. I have to measure my time now. I got to thinking that time given to others is maybe not honoring your own sacred time. I had to stop doing my tours because too many people didn't honor the sacred on them. Now I'm facing things I avoided. But I think pilgrimage is about how you find the sacred time. To do that you need a holy imagination—I'm convinced imagination is holy.

"In my youth," he concludes, "I thought the energies at sacred sites were my energies, but now I know they're old, and pilgrimage is a way for me to encounter those Old Currents. *You have to want to believe, to have faith.* Maybe it's about hunger, hunger for something deeper in my life."

Imagine ... it is wartime and your lover has been sent to prison. It is breath-crackling cold in the dead of winter as you wait with hundreds of others outside the prison walls for a word, a slip of paper from the authorities on why he was detained. Then a woman with nearly frost-bitten lips moves next to you, recognizes you, and whispers in your ear, "Can you describe this?"

When asked just this question, in a winter as brutal as that, the Russian poet Anna Akmatova replied: "Yes, I can."

"Then something that looked like a smile passed over what had once been her face."

How will you answer the voice who asks you now to describe what you are enduring halfway through your pilgrimage? For every time we move toward a significant goal, the world has a tendency to throw terrific obstacles in our way.

When Oliver Statler arrived at Temple Thirty-Nine on his circumambulation of eighty-eight shrines on Shikoku, the Buddhist priest there tried to assuage his misgivings about his journey: "The point of the pilgrimage is to improve oneself by enduring and overcoming difficulties."

THE GUIDING FORCE

*In the symbology of the labyrinth, Ariadne's thread
is the guiding force that leads Theseus to safety.*

—Lauren Artress

There is also a transcendent aspect to the labyrinth. Lauren Artress illustrates the exalted moments of using the labyrinth as part of one's spiritual practice in her book *Walking the Sacred Path*. She writes that the symbolism of the labyrinth has existed in nearly all traditions around the world. It can be found in the Kabbala as an elongated figure based on the number 11, as well as the Hopi medicine wheel and Tibetan sand paintings. Other traditions include variations on the labyrinth, such as the cosmic knot, the tattoos of South Seas peoples, the Celtic torque, the mystic poetry of the Sufis, and children's board and dance games.

What these models have in common is that they have been used for centuries as transformative tools. They symbolize an inner condition that people around the world share: solutions to what Artress calls "larger-than-life questions." These are spiritual issues, she points out, and "to seek answers to these questions is to seek a sacred path.

As we find our meaning and purpose we also realize that some invisible form of guidance has been leading us."

She weaves an illustration of this spiritual hunger with a retelling of George Macdonald's fairytale *The Princess and the Goblin:*

A young princess is sent away from her father's kingdom, away from the world, to a castle of supposed safety. She begins to explore her new home and encounters an old woman spinning thread in the tower. The woman introduces herself as the princess's great-grandmother. She tells the princess that she has awaited her princess for years. In time, the great-grandmother gives the princess a ring to which she attaches an invisible thread. This thread, the great-grandmother tells the princess, will guide her through the challenges she meets in life. The child is disappointed in her gift because she cannot see the thread or the ball that it comes from, which remains with the great-grandmother.

This wise old tale offers a hint of what it means to follow the sacred way through the labyrinth. Artress writes, "By following an invisible thread we connect to the Source, to the Sacred." But what can this thread possibly refer to? And why does it disappoint us at first? Learning to trust this invisible lead requires great faith. Artress calls the great-grandmother's magic thread "the God within." Another view is that it is an ancient symbol for the *soul* itself, the path taken through the ancestor's realm.

The medieval fascination for mazes and labyrinths faded over the centuries, but recently there has been a resurgence of interest in, using them as a meditation tool to still the mind and open the soul. A program at San Francisco's Grace Cathedral led by Artress is in the vanguard of the movement. Under her guidance, a replica of the Chartres labyrinth has been installed in front of the cathedral, and a woven version travels to churches and halls around the country. People of all faiths and persuasions are learning of the calming inspiration this ancient tool has on those who walk its sacred patterns.

Artress now lectures and leads pilgrimages to labyrinth sites around the world, reclaiming the labyrinth as a transformative tool for thousands of the spiritually hungry. For her, it is a multivalent symbol, representing the soul's journey through life as well as "an ancient symbol for the Divine Mother, the God within, the Goddess, the Holy in all of creation." Her belief is that the labyrinth is symbolic of the inner pilgrimage on which travelers can have

The sacred geometry of Grace Cathedral, San Francisco, accomplishes its ancient task by lifting the spirit as the eye follows the north tower into the clouds.

a "firsthand experience of the Divine." The ritual of circumambulation, she believes, carries on the ancient theme of the pilgrim's steady and winding movement toward the sacred center.

Jeannette Hermann was a participant in one of Artress' recent labyrinth tours through Europe and describes its impact this way:

When Lauren called me out of my seat to walk the labyrinth with the group, I figured I'd do it, get it over with, and get back to my work. All I know is, when I stepped into the labyrinth what was on my mind as the travel director of this group had been the lunch arrangements, the bus location, and departure time. I hadn't walked three steps before a long-forgotten crisis popped into my head, along with a very poignant question. I was stunned and, immediately torn from the mundane, began curiously probing this old wound. I remembered what Lauren said about passing people in front of you who were too slow, and taking your own route should you feel inclined. I thought I had surely stepped off the path, lost in my own reverie, and was never going to reach the center. I sighed and nodded my head as I dealt with that as another life metaphor. More questions came as if from beyond the pale and awakened an awareness in me. Tears began to flow. Things I'd kept hidden from myself all these years were in my face. By the grace of God I did reach the center and made my way out. When I sat down to absorb the experience, one of the women who had befriended me came to me with a notepad and pen. She said, "I was told to give you this as you want to write something." After saying I had my own pen and paper, I realized more was yet to come and accepted the offer. As I wrote, more was revealed to me, and when I finished, I began my dash to the restaurant only to meet the French guide in the vestibule. She had already taken care of lunch arrangements. This was my first group walk of a labyrinth, and by the end of the tour, I found each labyrinth had its own energy. Amiens was very personal; Chartres was more universal, opening my heart chakra. All I wanted to do was hug everybody. I found it very powerful, even if you are not looking for it.

FOLLOWING THE THREAD BACK

I have a feeling that my boat has struck, down in the depths,
against a very great thing.
—Juan Ramón Jiménez (1881–1958)

In some traditions of Buddhist practice, devotees each day acknowledge gratitude to parents, teachers, friends, and all other forms of life for their contributions toward the enrichment of their lives. As someone participating in the venerable tradition of sacred travel, pilgrims are expected to acknowledge gratitudes to their innkeepers, those who feed them, and their companions along the road.

What is far more difficult is be grateful for the hardships along the road. His Holiness the Dalai Lama has said, "If you utilize obstacles properly, then they strengthen your courage, and they also give you more intelligence, more wisdom." But if you use them in the wrong way, he adds, laughing gently, then you will feel "discouraged, failure, depression."

In that ritual action of taking a spiritual or mythological attitude toward the "sacrificial" circumstances of your journey, in the ancient manner of Theseus and Ariadne who had to "twist the threads" of their fate, is the way to make sacred your journey. As is often the case, the perennial truth of the idea is rooted in the word itself: *sacrifice* comes from the Latin *sacri-ficium*, which means "making sacred."

Imagine that your task in the labyrinth is to find the center. When in doubt, remember your original intention for the journey; recall your purpose; reinstate your vow; rekindle your fire by doing something passionate; rediscover the thread that led you to your pilgrimage in the first place.

Remember that the risks you took, the physical and spiritual dangers you've encountered, the financial and spiritual sacrifices you've made, were to rediscover what is most sacred in your life.

Without the thread you haven't got a *clew*.

THE SPLENDID PRISM OF LOVE

I stood at a crossroads and fate came to meet me....
—Liz Greene

W hen poet and screenwriter Richard Beban discovered that his father had cancer, he decided to take him on a pilgrimage to Paris. An *artist manqué* all his life, Beban's father longed to see "the home of artists," the source of the painting he loved most—the Impressionists. Though father and son experienced moments of transcendence in museums and cafés, it was not the easiest of journeys. Tension between them, the specter of death, the sometimes difficult weather—all conspired against Richard's dream of *rapprochement*. But Richard persevered, watching, waiting, writing, hoping for an opening.

Finally, he took his father shopping at the oldest market in Paris, and later that evening cooked him a simple meal. Afterward, he wrote down a few observations that became a poem called, "My Father and I Shopped."

> *in the street market*
> *along the rue Mouffetard*
> *amid the babble of accents,*
> *the recent immigrants:*
> *dark faces from North Africa,*
> *brown skins from Algeria,*
> *fragrant, ghost white mushrooms*

from the dark earth of Brittany
the ancient gray Parisians;
herbs and peppers and vegetables—
reds, greens, and yellows, each distinct,
luminous in the overcast.

When we returned to our rented flat
he napped, tired from the short walk.

I sliced two large tomatoes in rounds
drained them, picked basil,
dried the muted green leaves,
sliced the spongy white mozzarella,
remembering the way he sliced salami when I was young,
precise, paper-thin, an astonishing number of slices
from a single, stubby sausage.

On two white porcelain plates I interleaved
tomato, mozzarella, basil.

When I heard him in the bathroom, shaking out
the ration of pills that were buying him the extra days,
I drizzled golden olive oil over the salads,
set them on the table
with red linen napkins,
with polished silver.

Before he ate, he photographed the plate.

This marvelous poem is translucent in the way it depicts how we might all deal with sorrow on our journeys. Never doubt for a moment that there will be darkness and disappointment on your travels. The question is, How much courage can we muster to deal with it and move on? Can we transform painful moments into instructive ones? How quick are our reflexes?

The ancient Persians said, "If fate throws a knife at you, you can catch it either by the blade or the handle."

In *Mystery and Manners*, Flannery O'Connor writes, "No matter what form the dragon may take, it is the mysterious passage past him, or into his jaws, that stories of any depth will be concerned to tell."

Imagine the surprise of frontiersman Daniel Boone when he was asked if he had ever been lost. "No," he replied slyly. "But I was bewildered once for three days."

THE TRAVELER'S WELL

It's not the road ahead that wears you out—
it's the grain of sand in your shoe.
—old Arabian proverb

Leo Tolstoy was fond of an old eastern fable that describes the mysterious way that even tragedy lures us back to life. His story is about a traveler on the steppes who was surprised by a rampaging tiger. The traveler ran for his life, but the beast was gaining on him, so he leapt into a dried-up well, which roused a dragon that had been sleeping on the bottom. As the traveler fell, he was alert enough to grab on to a single, slim branch growing between the cracks of the bricks in the well. There he clung for his life—above him the tiger roaring, below him the dragon snapping its jaws. The traveler's arms grew tired, and he knew it was only a matter of time before the tiger swiped at him from above or he fell to his death.

Stubbornly, he held on. The moment he began to hope for a way out, he noticed two mice, one black, one white, gnawing away at either side of the tender branch he clung to. His time was almost up. Surely, he would die soon.

Then a glint of sunlight fell on the wall of the well. The traveler's eyes widened. There on the leaves of the bush were drops of honey. He felt a rush of happiness and with the few moments he had left, he calmly stretched out his tongue and tasted the precious honey.

Imagine the time you have spent working your way through the labyrinth of your travels. What was chasing you? What stares up at you from below?

Are there no drops of honey on the leaves right before your eyes?

CROSSING THE THRESHOLD

Place your mind before the mirror of eternity!
Place your soul in the brilliance of glory!
—Saint Clare of Assisi

In the summer of 1986, I entered Chartres Cathedral through the massive medieval doors and walked across the nave. My only companions were the silent storms of sunlight streaming through the stained-glass windows. The sound of my heart surged as I stood in the center of the ancient labyrinth.

Slowly, I followed the winding way over the black-and-white flagstones, a path worn smooth from 800 years of pilgrimages. Thirty-four turns on the meandering path later, I recrossed the threshold, buffeted by a strange wind.

An old Frenchman in a black felt beret was waiting for me. Uncannily, he reminded me of my great-grandfather Charlemagne. He tapped me on the arm with the crook of his oak walking cane. His were the eyes of a court jester, but bore the weariness of the wayward pilgrim. In deeply accented English, he asked me with the riddling power of a traveling bard, "Do you know where I can find God?"

I felt a cool shiver crawl down my spine, a peculiar prickling at the back of my neck. His eyebrows arched expectantly. I was completely bewildered. Was he a mad theologian? A sardonic existentialist? Could he be testing my knowledge of arcane architecture or medieval philosophy? He squinted, waited impatiently, as if there were words lurking in me that might surprise us both.

Suddenly, rays of blue light slanted in from the brilliantly bright rose window above the choir loft, landing warmly on my face. Only then did I realize I'd been waiting for this question all my life.

Casually, I pointed with my right thumb over my shoulder and down to the whorling pattern in the stone floor. The old man touched the edge of his beret, and bowed elegantly. Nodding with great relief as a sad Gallic sigh escaped out of the corner of his crinkled mouth, he stepped across the threshold and disappeared inside the ancient question, his cane keeping the time beyond time.

Imagine someone tapping you on the shoulder while you bask in reverie at a strange and marvelous church, mosque, or synagogue. He is whispering in your ear, "Where can I find God?"

Quick, what would you tell him?

VI
ARRIVAL

This is a great moment, when you see,
however distant, the goal of your wandering.
The thing which has been living in
your imagination suddenly becomes a part
of the tangible world.

—Freya Stark

FOR A THOUSAND YEARS, FROM AS FAR AWAY AS EGYPT, Italy, and Asia Minor, they came. Seekers from every walk of life, from peasants to kings, made the long journey across the plains of Thessaly to the slopes of Mount Parnassus in Greece to seek counsel with the Oracle at Delphi.

To reach the shrine demanded great effort on the part of the early pilgrims, but the rewards were immediate and sometimes life-altering. At the top of the long climb to the sanctuary, the traveler would have looked down over one the most breathtaking views in the world. Gasping at the richest treasures of any site in antiquity, the pilgrims would feel blessed by the gods for their good fortune in arriving safely at the most sacred sanctuary in the world.

Delphi was a cult center for the worship of Gaia, the earth goddess. It is said that her priestesses, called the Sibyls, uttered strange and terrifying prophecies. Legend has it that the very first one, Herophile, predicted the tragedy of the Trojan War. Later, the story was told that Apollo, god of light and reason, slew the python who had long guarded the site, and now gave counsel through his priestess.

On the slopes below the temple, pilgrims who wanted to consult with the Delphic Oracle first made a ritual sacrifice of a sheep, goat, or honeycake, then ritually washed in the Castalian Spring and climbed the Sacred Way to wait until summoned to the sanctuary. While they waited, pilgrims were free to wander through the olive groves or strike up conversations with priests or fellow pilgrims.

Over the gateway to the small sanctuary were etched the famous mottoes of Delphi: Socrates' own utterance *Know Thyself* and the folk saying *Everything in Moderation.* Through the gateway, the weary trav-

eler would enter the dark chamber within the temple that housed the
omphalos, a sculpted stone believed to be the center—the womb—of
the world. The prophetess, who had purified herself in the spring and
drunk from the sacred fountain, sat behind a curtain upon a gold tripod. There, she received the pilgrims' earnest entreaties in the form of
questions written on lead tablets.

Plato describes how the Pythia, as the Oracle was sometimes
called, would be overcome by a "prophetic madness," which poured
forth some "creative insight." She went into a trance, believed to be
inspired by a potent combination of the guardian god Apollo's blessings and the laurel leaves she chewed. The legendary vapors that reput-
edly rose from the crevice beneath the tripod have never been
discovered, but the wisdom that came from the Oracle's trances and
convulsions, the prophecies, spoken with enthusiasm (literally her
"being filled by a god"), are a window into the Greek soul. In a voice
husky and quavering, she addressed the pilgrim in the first person, giving the impression that Apollo himself was dispelling the advice. The
usually unintelligible answers were then transformed into hexameters
by the temple priests or a "poet-in-residence" lingering nearby. The
poetic interpretation was inevitably obscure and ambiguous, but still
considered to be the ultimate authority.

"The real secret lies in the riddling nature of the Oracle's
response," writes author and scholar Alexander Eliot. "They left a
wide margin for error, but that is not the main point. They opened up
the same margin for the sense of wonder to fill in." Rather than being
vague, as is often the charge, the Oracle answered in "certainties," but,
as Eliot recounts, her words always stressed the "underlying mysteries
of existence. So the eternal paradox of faith—certainty resting on mystery—seemed resolved at Delphi in some very direct way."

Although scholars debate how many of the oracular answers are
historically verified (current estimates number only seventy-five), the
lasting power of Delphi is in its grip on the imagination, its imposing

silent rebuttal of all mortal attempts to explain away its power to pene-
trate the soul. Those who walked or rode hundreds of miles bearing a
heavy question in their hearts, through dint of the ordeal and rituals
involved, invariably left with some form of soul-stirring vision. In a saga-
cious interpretation in his book *Earth, Air, Fire, and Water,* Elliot states,
"The more [the pilgrim] turned the riddle over in his mind, the more it
would become involved with his own deepest instincts and desires."

By definition, it takes a leap of faith to enter into the frame of mind
that can crack a riddle from such a source. One example will suffice to
illustrate the point: Croesus, the rich and mighty ruler of Lydia, traveled to Delphi to ask the Oracle if he should march on Persia.

"If Croesus crosses the river Aly a mighty empire will fall."

He marched and was crushed by Cyrus. In his haste and hubris he
forgot to ask which empire.

The journey to Delphi is emblematic of all pilgrimages. At a fundamental level, all pilgrimage sites are oracular. But we must be careful
how to frame the question and how to interpret the answer. We can
leave the most impressive of offerings behind, as the pilgrims did at
Delphi, in hopes of a favorable prophecy, but as we now know, the
Oracle never predicted. Instead, she offered an insight into the unfolding she saw taking place in the pilgrim's soul.

If we leave home with a fundamental question in our hearts and
minds, we are moving toward an oracular encounter, the "sacred wellspring," the source where we can replenish our lives.

Each time we enter a cathedral wondering what role faith plays in
our lives, or wander the halls of a museum pondering how much we
need beauty, we are experiencing the everyday influence of the Oracle.
The ambiguous messages we hear from the pulpit, the artist's studio,
or the poet's garret are modern counterparts of the cryptic messages of
the Delphi Oracle. Invariably, sages will turn the riddle back on us. The

intensity of our questioning, the willingness to puzzle it out until the answer is revealed, speaks to the oracular power that is possible at any site we have reached after a long and risky pilgrimage.

What is important about a shrine is not what can be documented by historians but what has transpired in the hearts of pilgrims. As Diane Skafte writes in *Finding the Oracles*, "They came because something *happened* to them there. Oracular presence changes everything it touches, and this presence must have been powerful in a site where oracles had lived for centuries. Hearing the oracle-speaker's actual words was only a small portion of the gift they received."

Imagine yourself arriving at Delphi 2,500 years ago. What sacrifice did you make to sanctify this voyage? How did you purify yourself? What gifts have you bought for the treasury? What question do you have in store for the Oracle? This moment is the joy of your heart's desire, and the source of the power that lured you here. How will you honor it?

On the morning of the day of your arrival at the sacred site that was the goal of your journey, recall what the prophecies have said in your dreams, in the sacred books you read to prepare for this auspicious moment. Try to see everything around you at this moment as portentous—the birdsong outside your window, the light on the olive groves, the way the clouds have formed over the mountains in the distance. Sit in bed a few extra minutes with your eyes closed. You have risen earlier than usual, from anticipation. Pay close attention to any dreams still frothing on the surface of your mind. Is there something welling up inside you that has flamed into dream? Before you do anything else, read a few lines from a book you consider spiritually appropriate for your visit to the shrine. On a visit to Delphi it could be some fragments of poetry by the sublime Sappho:

You may forget but
Let met tell you
this: someone in
some future time
will think of us.

At sites such as Delphi, Epidaurus, Konya, Ephesus, places where the collective dreamings of pilgrims over the centuries produces a hyp-

notic effect in the air, it is a small good thing to pray upon rising. This takes different forms for different people. Perhaps a traditional prayer, a chant from a hymn book, the repetition of a mantra or *gatha*, one of the sayings of the Buddha. Whatever is holy to you, whatever brings you peace as you start the day is prayerful.

The next small good thing is to prepare a question for the day. Each morning, write a few lines in your journal that you want to meditate on

The author regales fellow pilgrims Barbara Haigh, and Sue Beaton with the passionate feelings that the amphitheater around them has evoked for many centuries, Epidaurus, Greece.

during the day. It's wonderful to focus your thoughts during a time that is supposed to be sacred. Next bear in mind a bare-bones day. Simplify, simplify, simplify. Eat simply, dress simply, care little. If possible, find some sacred music to listen to, perhaps in a local church or chapel. These are simple soul-stretches, humble exercises that can inch us forward toward that pure moment of arrival. These practices help ready the heart for that unique joy, but no guide, no guidebook, can hand you the sacred experience.

"No one can bring you peace but yourself," as Emerson reminded his audiences. But there, in the echo of inspired words—are those qualities to which we aspire: love, happiness, peace—drawing us closer and closer to the longed-for truth of our journey; that we are forever trying to get to our true home.

THE HEARTBEAT OF THE WORLD

You enter Greece as one might enter a dark crystal; the form of things becomes irregular, refracted. . . . Other countries may offer you discoveries in manner of lore or landscape; Greece offers you something harder—the discovery of yourself.
—Lawrence Durrell, *Greece*

When I think of sacred journeys, the word *ineffable* comes to mind. The experiences that travelers have at Delphi, Avebury, Bodh Gaya, are often unspeakable, seemingly impossible to put into words. But occasionally, someone finds the words to describe the way a place can strike awe in the heart of the pilgrim. One scene comes to mind from Henry Miller's account of his journey to Greece. *The Colossus of Marousi* is a book that streamed from the heavens straight into the soul of its author. The morning dew of rural Greece seeped into his pen as he conveyed the peace that reigns at fugitive moments in those ancient hills.

Miller's pilgrimage began with a simple conversation with a woman friend in Paris, was nudged along by a series of letters from his friend, author Lawrence Durrell, and then ignited by a conversation with a Greek medical student. Traveling through Greece brought about a shift in his soul and his writing style, moving from the priapic style of the *Tropic* books of the Paris years, to the epiphanic, in which he begins to describe "something beyond bliss," the way that "marvelous things happen to one in Greece—marvelous good things. . . ."

His journey unfolded into a serendipitously sacred one. His path-way to the center goes through the "Colossus," a Greek named Katsimbalis. As limned by Miller, he is a sublime monologist who embodied the Greek miracle of seeing the light of creation everywhere. So infused with life is he that after their encounter, Miller sets off to visit the sacred sites of the Peloponnesus. Miller describes the pilgrims who made the long journey to Epidaurus as being cured before they ever arrived—an echo of the ancient belief that the very act of pilgrimage triggers a healing. When he finally arrives, he walks to the "strangely silent amphitheater" and ponders the circuitous route he took to arrive there, the labyrinth he had been caught in for thirty years, never know-ing peace, nor realizing that the Minotaur had been himself.

> As I entered the still bowl, bathed now in a marble light, I came to that spot in the dead center where the faintest whisper rises like a glad bird and vanishes over the shoulder of the low hill, as the light of a clear day recedes before the velvet black of night. . . .
>
> Epidaurus is merely a place symbol: the real place is in the heart, in every man's heart, if he will but stop and search it. Every dis-covery is mysterious in that it reveals what is so unexpectedly immediate, so close, so long and intimately known. The wise man

*has no need to journey forth; it is the fool who seeks the pot of
gold at the rainbow's end. But the two are always fated to meet
and unite. They meet at the heart of the world, which is the
beginning and the end of the path. They meet in realization and
unite in transcendence of their roles.*

For Miller, like the pilgrims of old, the experience of that stillness
brought a personal revelation and began the longed-for healing. It
brings on a feeling of sweet veneration. Anaïs Nin has described
Miller's uncanny talent for missing nothing on his walks around Paris,
noticing everything on the surface of life. But at Epidaurus, he was
introduced to the depths that pulse below the surface.

This is one of the perennial messages in quest stories—that of
gaining entry into the temple, reaching the sacred center after an arduous journey—and is symbolic of death and rebirth. For Miller,
Epidaurus was a balm, a cure for his aching heart and soul. Another
traveler might see nothing but scattered ruins and be unable to fill in
the gaps of stone and story with imagination. But for the initiated,
there is unabashed wonder and humbleness before the sacred. It's as if
you've surprised the secret lurking at the heart of the world.

Imagine that you have arrived alone at the sanctuary. You will most
likely have great crowds to deal with. How will you let them affect you?
If you truly want to experience the venerable sites of antiquity alone—
go off-season. These sites were chock-a-block long before you were born
and will be long after the current tourist wave washes away. With some
self-discipline, it is possible to learn the grace moves of dealing with
large, gawking crowds. Try to see yourself as an ancient traveler. Prepare
by reading accounts of travelers who have passed this way before you.

If you are with a group, find a kindred spirit. It can ruin a day at the ruins to be with someone who doesn't like old stones or tires easily of museums. The upside of group tours are that they provide an opportunity for community, which many spiritual leaders and anthropologists like Victor Turner consider to be one of the main points of pilgrimage.

By their nature, pilgrimages are a confluence of many peoples from many cultures. Everyone has a fear of fribbling away time and a desire for the authentic.

Practice patience. Think of others as fellow seekers.

THE MOMENT OF TRUTH

If you miss the moment, you miss your life.
—John Daido Loori

Bettina Selby began in London as an unbeliever, an agnostic, and pedaled her bicycle a thousand miles along the old pilgrim's trail to the "Field of the Star," the shrine at Santiago de Compostela. She arrived transformed.

"The journey was not something outside time and reality," she writes in *Pilgrim's Road*, "but an opportunity to look at the same realities from a different angle and in a different context." She candidly admits that she did not "for a moment believe that St. James had ever set foot in Spain, dead or alive.... But there are strange powers attached to places that cannot be rationally explained." She cites the Hebrides, the monasteries of eastern Turkey, Lindisfarne, but also those sites "of really hideous deeds" as having a sense of "presence."

The moment that "finally made a real if reluctant pilgrim" of her reflects the humility learned on the pilgrim's road. She heard the traditional request *Priez pour nous*, "Pray for us," again and again from people along the road. There was an unspoken belief that she would gain a certain power by completing her journey. Her biggest fear, however, was that the end of her journey would be anticlimactic. But as she ped-aled her bicycle down the final blocks and into Santiago, she realized that it was "the jewel in the crown" of her pilgrimage. It thrilled her to shift her months-long solitude into a sense of communion with the thousands of fellow pilgrims who gathered in "one of the noblest squares in Europe," near the cathedral. She followed the hallowed rit-ual of "climbing the stone stairs and passing under the Portico de la Gloria, past the threshold and into the cathedral to view the relics of St. James.... What the newly arrived pilgrims see, exalted as they are at the end of the trek, and by all the magnificence and beauty they have already seen in the approach to their goal, is the pool of warm golden light drawing them on."

As described in the original *Pilgrim's Guide*, arrival at the Cathedral of Santiago de Compostela has always been a complex ritual. Originally, the pilgrims went to pay respects at the apostle's tomb as soon as they arrived; then they attended Mass in the cathedral, which included offerings for candles and oil. As William Metczer points out in his study on the eight-century history of the pilgrimage, "With the passing of a few generations, however, more elaborate practices were devised to ensure a more efficient and uniform flow of cash." An all-night wake plus confession and Holy Communion were added to the ritual arrival as preparation for the actual visit to the tomb. Cathedral officials hovered nearby with an offering chest to prompt pilgrims to add to the coffers and complete their own duties.

Later, the arrival ritual focused on the display, touching, and wit-nessing of the relics. The centerpiece was "a glittering chest of aston-ishing marvels," and then veneration of the remains of St. James in the vaulted tombs ... constituted moments of the highest reverberation for the pilgrim, moments that he would henceforth cherish and, jealously

One of the prime forces of pilgrimage is the desire to see or touch the relic of a revered saint or hero. The handbones of St. John the Baptist are displayed at the Topkapi Museum in Istanbul, Turkey.

guarded, take back with him to his village or town and actually down into his grave.... [K]neeling in front of the reliquary that treasured the remains of St. James ... the pilgrims sank in thought and prayer that more often than not included some long-guarded personal wish for a miraculous intervention of the saint."

Selby's arrival surprised her. Before the glittering altar with its silver casket of relics she felt less in awe of the relics than of the "spot where all those who had asked me to pray for them would wish me to do so. ... The St. James who was enshrined here, the St. James I had gradually become aware of on the pilgrimage, was what had come from the hearts and minds of the thousands and thousands of people who had walked the *Camino de Santiago*, for all these hundreds of years, struggling with meanings, with conscience, with faith and with the lack of it."

FACING THE BLACK STONE

Zamzam water is for the end for which one drinks it.
If you drink it for a cure, it will cure you; to fill your stomach,
it will satisfy you; and if to ease a burning thirst, it will quench it."
—Kitab al-Kawkab al-Durri

W hen Ibn Battua of Morocco finally arrived in Mecca he was fascinated by the beating of drums each morning and deeply impressed with the kindness of the locals whose custom it was to share one-third of their food with the poor. He described the ritual of daily prayers and prostrations, the ritual processions to kiss the Black Stone at the center of the shrine:

"As the imam prepares to mount the steps, the muezzin gives him the sword, and the imam strikes the first step with it. This draws the attention of the crowds. He does the same with the other steps and strikes the fourth time at the top. Next, he prays in a low voice, facing the Ka'ba, then turns to the public, bowing to this right and left. The congregation returns the gesture. At the very moment that he sits down, the muezzin begins the call to prayer, standing on the dome of the Zamzam Well."

Many sojourners come and stay on at Mecca for many years. Among those who impressed Ibn Battua with their piety was a Sufi devotee known as al-Yafi'i.

"This man was almost constantly circling the Ka'ba 'by night and at the odd hours of the day.' Often, after performing his evening cir-cuits, he would climb to the roof of the Muzaffariya college and sit there watching the Ka'ba until he fell asleep. He would place a flat stone beneath his head and rest a little, then renew his ablutions [*wudu'*] and take up his circling again until the time came for the morning prayer...."

Battua noticed another pilgrim, Shaykhy Abu al-Abbas ibn Marzug, the "most determined in circling the Ka'ba. His persistence in spite of the heat always amazed me, for the pavement around the shrine is flagged with black stones and the midday sun heats them up like red-hot plates. I have seen the water bearers attempt to wet them down, but no sooner does the water hit the stone than the spot changes color and starts steaming. Most people performing the *tawaf* [ritual circuit] at that hour wear sandals, but this man did it with bare feet."

CIRCLING THE SACRED CENTER

This was the moment. I felt the thrilling moment of destiny.
—James P. Carse

For the Celts the world is, as John O'Donoghue writes in *Anam Cara*, "always latently and actively spiritual." Since time immemorial, there has been a belief that language is one power that can tap, even trigger, "divine events," and that pilgrimage, what was called in old Gaelic *turas*, ritual circuits, was a way to participate in the flow of energy between the two worlds.

Peter Harbison writes in his history of Irish pilgrimage, "For Ireland, pilgrimage is a pious exercise that has helped to fulfill religious needs and yearnings for more than 1,400 years." Several forms of pilgrimage have flourished there. There was the *ascetic*, which meant leaving behind one's land forever to embark on a life-until-death pilgrimage, and there was the *penitential*, undertaken to expiate sin. Probably the most famous of all is the pilgrimage to Croagh Patrick, the celebrated mountain where Saint Patrick was believed to drive the snakes from Ireland. Harbison cites the early voyages of Saint Brendan and Columcille, described in contemporary annals already as pilgrimages.

Formerly, the *tura* proceeded up the old Tochar Phadraig, the old pilgrimage trackway, and the ascent began at midnight. With only lamp, candle, or flashlight, and perhaps a shillelagh or ashplant walking stick, the pilgrim walked barefoot on the sharp stones near the top. At the first station, the stones known as Saint Benen's Bed, the pilgrim circles seven times while praying; at the summit, the pilgrim prays while circling the new chapel, then goes to Mass and takes Holy Communion.

Today, the practice of *turas* around saints' tombs, pre-Christian sites, and holy wells while praying or singing in the belief of restoring the soul, flourishes. In Celtic mythology, the god of the sea, Manannan mac Lir, said, "No one will have knowledge who does not drink from the well." Seen as the entranceways to the world below, wells have long been regarded sacred in Ireland and are a potent symbol for the power believed to lurk in all holy sites.

Father Stephen Canny, an Irish priest who leads a parish in Santa Rosa, California, is a firm believer in pilgrimage. He has climbed Croagh Patrick three times himself and has seen it work wonders on the devoted. "You are more *alive* after you have overcome something difficult," he says. "You're changed by the mountain and the fact that you have confirmed your faith. It's a remarkably effective way to answer the question, *What is my purpose?*"

A HAIKU JOURNEY

Do not seek to follow in the footsteps of the men of old,
seek what they sought."
—Matsuo Basho

For some travelers the meaning of a pilgrimage is in the moment of arrival. For others, the meaning is in the journey itself, where every step reveals a piece of the answer being sought. The seventeenth-century poet-pilgrim Matsuo Basho is one of the supreme

This ukiyo-e *image of two Japanese travelers making their way through the snow evokes the spirit of the poet-pilgrim Basho. By Utagawa Hiroshige (1797–1858)*

examples of this tradition. "The passing days and months are eternal travelers in time," he wrote in his most famous book, *A Narrow Road to Far Places.* "The years that come and go are travelers too. Life itself is a journey...."

From the age of twenty-two until his death in 1694, Basho devoted himself body and soul to his two passions: writing poetry and going on pilgrimages to the places written about by the immortal Japanese poets. "There will be hardships enough to make my hair white," he wrote before he set off from Soka, "but I shall see with my own eyes places about which I have only heard! I shall be fortunate if I but return alive, I thought, staking my future on that uncertain hope."

We hear in this desire to "see with my own eyes" the dreams of pilgrims all over the world. Basho's peripatetic life embodied his Buddhist belief that existence is a "pilgrim's progress." According to legend, he inscribed on his pilgrim's hat the words *Kenkon muju; doko ninin*— "Homeless I wander, in company with God."

Homeless he was, after selling his house to finance his pilgrimage, but he found a home each night in the bittersweet fashion of pilgrims the world over. His travel journals have been required reading for pilgrims for three centuries. They reveal that there doesn't have to be only one arrival. For Basho, each encounter of his five-month journey, each shrine, each inn, was an arrival to be celebrated in verse with his characteristically sensual attention to the details of the moment. I find in his remarkable observations the simplest of guidelines for a journey inspired by soulful attention.

At Sukagawa, "the quietness and solitude" remind him of a poem by Saigyo, so he *responds* to the soul of the moment by taking out paper and ink brush and first commenting on the ideographs and symbolism of the poem, then writing his own. At Takekuma, he marvels at a famous pine tree that has branched off into twin trunks. His associative mind similarly branches off and he is reminded of the tenth-century poet-priest Noin who had written of the same tree six centuries before. Upon leave-taking, he and his traveling companion compose poetry for each other, in honor of their visit. At Sendai, he walks with a local poet to discover "places nearby mentioned in poetry, traces of which had almost disappeared, but which he found after much searching." Then, at Tobu Castle, he leaves us the key to the way of his imagination. Speaking of a famous stone there, Basho writes, "This monument was made a thousand years ago and is a very real and vivid link with the past. Seeing it is one of the things that has made my trip worthwhile and one of the happiest moments of my life. Forgetting all the trials of the journey, I wept for sheer joy."

This passage reveals the charm of Basho's book, his approach to travel, and his devotion to pilgrimage. The poet-pilgrim admits that he "could not help marveling" about shrines, temples, poetic ballads, or

A traditional print by an unknown artist of the Buddhist saint Kobo Daishi, depicted as a pilgrim with bamboo monk's hat, walking staff, and begging bowl. Basho would have worn similar clothes, as do many modern Japanese pilgrims.

the "profound tranquillity and beauty" of a place that somehow makes his heart feel "deeply purified."

That and his willingness to be able to say that he "savored the melancholy beauty," what the Japanese call *sabi*, the "sigh of the moment," of a scene, an encounter, a recollection.

In this bush profound,
Into the very rocks it seeps—
The cicada sound.

In the seventeen syllables of this traditional Japanese haiku, Basho compresses the art of pilgrimage, the skill of observation, the soul of attention, and the heart of intention. All well and good for a wandering pilgrim of centuries past, the modern traveler might well say, but what about *me*? How might *I* see with such tenderness, feel with such depth, especially when the road has taken so much of me by the time I've arrived at my destination?

Like many other great souls, Basho never gave direct answers. His reflections are like a stilled pond; his words nudge us toward our own stillness.

"Make the universe your companion," he wrote, "always bearing in mind the true nature of all creation—mountains and rivers, trees and grasses, and humankind...."

Imagine what it was the wise ones sought on the journey you are now re-creating. Was it "the hush profound," the companionship of nature, the blessing of the ancient ones as you leave your own unique footsteps? Try to see how practicing that kind of devotion might help you learn to see and feel the vital forces in yourself and in the certain sacred sites.

Think of poet-pilgrims like Basho as embodying the art of seeing, of noticing. In his words, we are reminded of the role of spirituality in travel: the *inward* experience while traveling *outward* along the roads of the world. Rather than constrict the mind, as so many modern travelers fear, the spiritual quest allows freer play of the imagination. His intention was not mindless respect for the past, but mindful attention to the myriad connections that past poets made. Enduring "agonizing stages of self-scrutiny," he achieved a rare depth of wisdom by concentrating on the eternals, what is constant and stands against the vicissitudes of time.

Try to recall an image of humbleness that has moved you on your journey, such as the empty alms bowl of a monk, the staff of an old hiker in the mountains as it touched the earth, or the voices of the choir at an open-air concert of medieval music.

We learn by going where we have to go; we arrive when we find ourselves on the road walking toward us.

THE STILL POINT

We must be still and still moving
Into another intensity....
—T. S. Eliot, *East Coker*

I n the summer of 1973, the poet James Wright and his wife Anne visited Italy. Like Goethe, Dickens, Lawrence, and millions before them, they found themselves revived by the simple elegance of life there.

"All I need at bottom is a small, uncluttered place," Wright wrote, "and of course a little pasta and a little sleep and the security of the people I care about."

While in Italy, he spent time in solitude with his notebooks. In them, he observed the shape, the secret light, the strangeness of stone, the sight of women working in groves, trying to seize what he called "the language of the present moment," in his own words and those of others. He described walking while reciting Dante out loud, feeling the muscles and veins rippling in ever-widening circles, "like a bird in flight under your tongue."

Under the ferocious noon sun in the amphitheater of Verona, built by the Romans a thousand years ago, he hears the voices of the ancient Italians and his own friends of twenty years past, then reflects, like Dante in the *Commedia*, of being seized midway on the road of life. He writes a note to his wife:

> *Today, in the middle of my own life, I woke beside the Adige [river].*
>
> *We hurried through breakfast for once, because the sun was splendid, and we wanted to enter the Arena and to walk all the way around it.*

Stolen moments of contemplation are the grace notes of a pilgrimage, such as a walk through a garden or cloister like this one at the twelfth-century Le Thoronet Abbey, Provence, France.

We climbed and stood as far away from each other as we could get without falling off the rim, as Amerigo Vespucci might have done. Far away I could see her, tiny and blazing in her golden skin, her wide-brimmed straw hat fluttering, one feather of one wing, still ascending. Instantly, we came home. I was impatient to write to you, because I do not want to waste time.

If there is a lovelier description of the holiness of time and longing for the beloved, I am not familiar with it. In this one humble note, Wright reflects on his role of poet as praise-singer, and of pilgrim as a recognizer of sacred time. Often in my own travels, I have sworn off an afternoon nap because I recalled Wright's sun-dappled letter, and so tromped back out onto the streets to find one more thing I may have missed, smelled one more aroma I'd never smelled before, or, simply, to feel my heart leap by witnessing a sunset from an unusual place.

There is joy at the heart of things.

Long before she wrote her first novel, *O Pioneers!*, Willa Cather took the abbreviated version of the Grand Tour of Europe, sending back numerous travel essays to the *Nebraska State Journal*. Her ultimate inspiration came from the French countryside, especially the village of Le Lavandou in the Dordogne:

> Out of every wandering in which people and places come and go in long successions, there is always one place remembered above the rest because the external or internal conditions were such that they most nearly always produced happiness. I am sure that for me that one place will always be Lavandou. Nothing else in England or France has given anything like this sense of immeasurable possession and immeasurable content. I am sure I do not know why a wretched little fishing village, with nothing but green pines and blue sea and a sky of porcelain, should mean more than a dozen places that I have wanted to see all my life. No books have ever been written about Lavandou, no music or pictures ever came from here, but I know well enough that I shall yearn for it long after I have forgotten London and Paris. One cannot divine or forecast the conditions that will make happiness; one only stumbles upon them by chance, in a lucky hour, at the world's end somewhere, and holds fast to the days, as to fortune or fame.

Here, in one paragraph, is the essence of arrival. Cather has perfected both directions of the art of attention. She *sees* the village, apprehends its bittersweet setting in the world, and she also sees into her own hidden heart. Then she basks in the glow of her immediate response to it. Her expressions of happiness feel like the gentlest zephyrs of the sea. Her words are as simple and mildly enviable as those of a wistful postcard sent by friend who has found a slice of paradise for a short period of time. Reading makes us wonder, *Where is my Lavandou? And if I find it, what can I do to remember it?*

THE ART OF WAKING UP

Thrice happy are those who have seen the Mysteries.
—Sophocles (496–408 B.C.E.)

O ne of the ancient functions of pilgrimage is to wake us from our slumber. Michigan artist Mary Rezmerski describes how an autumn solstice pilgrimage to Greece and Turkey that I led in 1992 helped her deal with the grief of her mother's death a few years before. Intuitively, rather than from logic, she packed some of her mother's things as talismans or amulets to take with her on her pilgrimage. The most important item was a very small hand mirror, "something small that held my mother's face within it; something so small yet capable of showing truth."

> *Our group journeyed to the ruins and sanctuary of the Mysteries of Eleusis. This contained the Sanctuary of Demeter. Demeter is the goddess whose daughter, Persephone, was abducted by Hades, the god of the underworld. Demeter searched and searched for her daughter; she looked everywhere. But her searches and her dark nights of the soul shed no light. When my mother died of cancer, she too was abducted. I searched and searched for her. But only when I went on the pilgrimage did I find her. I had to become a wayfarer in the darkness of my own soul. It happened because a guest lecturer on our tour, Carol Christ, the author of* Laugher of Aphrodite, *led us to a grotto. We gathered around its opening and listened as Carol read from her latest work about her own*

mother's recent death. This moment convinced me that pilgrimage unleashes synchronicity. Her eloquent emotions about the joy and terror of the mother-daughter bond touched deep chords in me. My sadness released my tears and I was able to openly cry and grieve. Carol's words celebrated her own relationship within the myth of the goddess Demeter and her daughter. Back at the hotel I looked deeply within my mother, Gloria's, mirror. For the first time I saw myself. I know Gloria held the mirror up for me to see myself.

This story is a remarkable example of the healing power of pilgrimage. Caught in the pain of grief and sorrow, Mary followed her intuition and risked a great deal in order to take a pilgrimage to a place she had read about since she was a girl. Her dreams told her something significant would happen there. She embarked on the journey with deep intention—to find some peace about her mother's death and to be reinspired as an artist. She prepared like a pilgrim: She prayed, she created a ritual departure beforehand by celebrating with friends and family, and she read prodigiously, so that when she arrived at the different sites along the pilgrimage she could exult in the "thrill of recognition."

In different eras and in a variety of ways, pilgrims have experienced the secret healing at Eleusis, that rare ecstasy from a group ritual that divines individual meaning. For this traveler, the words spoken on the sacred grounds were darts straight into her heart. She was initiated into the underworld of death and felt the joy of released grief. Originally, the Eleusian mysteries revealed a fateful attitude toward death with an accompanying assumption of transformation. Hence, the moment of truth in the rites was a presentation of a sheaf of wheat, the symbol of resurrection.

Shortly after our discussion with Carol Christ, we happened to walk past a sarcophagus near the Eleusis archaeological museum. Turning to Mary, I gently pointed out the way the stone tomb symbolized the entire Greek attitude toward death. Though *sarcophagus* means "flesh-eater," alluding to the decay over time in the tomb, the Greeks carved *psycheins*, butterflies, on their sides. The ancient symbol of transformation, and "the winged flight of the soul."

A lovely light danced on Mary's face as she ran her fingertips across the ancient carving.

THE PRESENCE OF PLACE

I will study and get ready, and maybe the chance will come.
—Abraham Lincoln

Anthropologist Jay Fikes vividly describes a visit to the Lincoln Memorial in Washington, D.C. as an extraordinary opportunity to fulfill a long-held desire to pay respects to one of his boyhood heroes. In the summer of 1995, after attending a memorial for the Winnebago medicine man Reuben Snake, Fikes drove with his wife and daughter from St. Louis, Missouri, to Springfield, Illinois, to see the tomb of Abraham Lincoln. He wanted his daughter to learn and experience American history in a way she couldn't do in her school-books. He says he wanted "to feel the *presence* of the place." At Springfield, they went to a historical center he describes as "cavelike, as if going back to a womb of history, returning to something primordial." When he emerged and saw the dioramas and read the plaques commemorating Lincoln, including the Gettysburg Address he had memorized as a boy, tears streamed down his face.

> *The passage prepared me for the climax of the place regarding somebody I do revere because he really paid a price for living out his ideals. The risk the hero takes; the hero sacrifices individuality and takes risk for a vision that transforms society if people act on*

it. While inside the exhibition, I asked a man who had been impersonating Lincoln why the president had commuted the Indians after the Santee Sioux uprising of 1862. There was no good hunting on the reservation. Some young Lakota took some food and the uprising began. After the Lakota were defeated, some 392 were tried, most for murder or rape; 303 Lakota were sentenced to hang. President Lincoln commuted the death sentence of all but 38 of these Lakota who had been sentenced to die by the military commission. Lincoln knew there was insufficient evidence to convict them and thus he refused to be railroaded by the popular dogma that the only good Indian was a dead Indian. The citizens of Minnesota were upset by Lincoln's pro-Indian decision to commute. The anti-Indian feeling was overwhelming. The fact that Lincoln had the courage to do what was right for the Lakota made me feel proud.

When the Lincoln impersonator explained his decision I felt my struggle to defend NACNA religious freedom had some historical ties.

Lincoln symbolizes what is best about America, our national creed that all humans are worthy of respect and that their rights to equal protection under the law to freedom of religion must be safeguarded by our federal government. I felt sad that he had been assassinated and left the tomb with an appreciation for our nation's most beloved president and a renewed commitment to our American ideals.

For Fikes, a committed pacifist and scholar intensely involved in preserving the religious freedom of native people in the United States and Mexico, Abraham Lincoln, more than any other American, symbolizes the qualities he most values.

Like a pilgrim of old, it was profoundly important for him to visit Lincoln's birthplace, view the "relics" of his life, and feel the ineffable sense of *presence* at the tomb and house. Moreover, it was an opportunity to express gratitude and come full circle with a vow he had made early in his life—to dedicate himself to the ideals of his country, which he still ardently believes are embodied in Lincoln.

James Van Harper is a comedian and actor living outside Birmingham, Alabama. All his life he has been inspired by the life of Elvis Presley. Two years after he and his wife Carmen married, he decided he needed to share his passion for the King of Rock 'n' Roll. On Valentine's Day in 1998, they visited Graceland.

The sixties and seventies were an exciting time for us Southern boys. From his first appearance on the Ed Sullivan Show to the times I played his 45 rpms to psyche myself up before football games, he was the man. He was the poor man who made good on his talent, turned it to pure gold. He knew what it was to sweat, to make a dollar. He had what it took to make women swoon. His face was white but he had the soul equal to any of the black pioneers of blues and jazz. Elvis forged his soul on the fire of Beale Street and in Tupelo, Mississippi. His birthplace was small, just south of Memphis. When we first visited Graceland, I enjoyed it but I was a little nervous. Because he was one of my greatest heroes. I was caught up being there, watching other people from all over the world come to be so close to him. A woman from Japan kept saying over and over how beautiful he was, how much he looked like her father.

I was really moved to see people from all over the globe there to see a good old Southern boy like me and the guys I grew up with. It wouldn't surprise me if in 200 years there was a new religious sect called The Elvites. Their robes would be jeweled jumpsuits, services would be two hours long, the length of his concerts, with encore prayers. A priest would raise the holy sacra-ments: Southern moon-pie, RC Cola, and finger sandwiches.

Harper is impassioned when he compares his need to acknowledge to himself the true soulfulness of Presley's creativity to the need he saw in poets and writers to cross the ocean to visit the famous shrines of their literary heroes. He suggests that his pilgrimage to the shrine was a chance to get close to the "relics" of the King of Rock 'n' Roll, because they might have a magical effect on his own creative dream.

"Not only was he was one of my heroes, I wanted to reach out and feel closer to my *wife*," he stresses. "By sharing my respect for him with her, I thought she might finally understand where my passion comes from, all the way back to my youth."

He adds that hearing Presley's songs takes him back to a precious time in his life: "Wow, that music is a touchstone of another era for me, I've told my wife Carmen. *That's* where I learned hope, that hope still abounds, that you can still fight for your dreams. Elvis also taught me that the only lasting thing is what we do for others. It's hard to put my finger on it, but I felt a kind of healing just being there at Graceland. Maybe I'm living vicariously through his legend, but see-ing how he lived for his family—not just his fans—reminded me that family is paramount. In a strange way it made me want to be closer to my own family!"

When asked what influence his visit to Graceland had on him, Harper replies, "My pilgrimage taught me that no matter what heights we reach, we all have struggles. It's magical, but being there at Graceland somehow allows me to carry my burden with a little more grace."

THE LITERARY PILGRIM

Blessings on the head of Cadmus or the Phoenicians,
or whoever it was that invented books.
—Thomas Carlyle

In 1995, Lawrence Ferlinghetti, poet, painter, publisher, and co-founder of City Lights Bookstore in San Francisco, received the Lifetime Achievement Award from the Bay Area Book Reviewer's Association. The keynote speaker that evening was Jon Carroll, columnist for the *San Francisco Chronicle*. In his speech, he recalled the pilgrimage he made to that touchstone bookstore when Carroll was a young man aspiring to the lofty goals of literary accomplishment.

Ferlinghetti was, as far as I can remember, the first non-assigned poet I ever read; I can still remember the dangerous radiance that the narrow black paperback of A Coney Island of the Mind *gave off as it sat on the bookshelf next to whatever it was next to, probably* The Prophet *or* Stranger in a Strange Land. *I took a bus from Monterey to San Francisco to sit in the basement of City Lights and wait for Ferlinghetti to walk in and notice my poetic soul.*

"You are my new friend," he would say, talking without contractions the way residents of Cannery Row were forever doing. "You must come to my home and we will drink red wine and read poetry all night and sleep with women." Alas, I sat in City Lights for hours and no one invited me to anything. It may have been my own dangerous radiance, which was not so much a Coney Island of the Mind *as a* Walnut Creek of the Spirit. *I passed the time, as I recall, reading the notices pinned to the bulletin board by the stairs—Wanted, ride to New York; will share*

> gas money. If I had had more courage and an automobile, I
> would have gladly thrown it all over and become, as I called it
> then, a Dharma Bum. Perhaps if I'd been clearer on the meaning
> of the word Dharma, things would have been different.

One afternoon in spring 1998, I was having lunch at one of my
neighborhood cafés, the Steps of Rome, near City Lights Bookstore,
and just happened to be contemplating the legacy of literary pilgrimage
when Ferlinghetti walked in. I invited him over to my table and, without missing a beat, asked him what he thought about the power of pilgrimage in regard to poetry and literature. He smiled and recited by
heart a few lines from his own "Adieu A Charlot" poem:

> The old generations have lived them out
> Lived out the bohemian myth in Greenwich Villages
> Lived out the Hemingway myth
> in The Sun Also Rises...

For a few minutes, he chronicled other literary pilgrimages, writers
walking in the footsteps of Henry Miller in Paris, D. H. Lawrence in
Mexico, and Jack Kerouac on the holy roads of America, concluding
with the image of the noble Tramp, Charlie Chaplin (Charlot, as the
French call him) who he feels is now is hidden inside the souls of
people he sees on every street corner.

Then Ferlinghetti suddenly recalled something he had been told
during one of his trips to the Czech Republic. "The ones running the
new art and literary scene now are former resistance members," he
remembered fondly. "They told me that during the Russian
Occupation, San Francisco poets and City Lights Bookstore were like a
light on the horizon for the people on the underground literary scene."

His blue eyes beamed. He nodded like a maestro, sipped his wine,
and ordered lunch.

For filmmaker John Antonelli, a trip to Lowell, Massachusetts, in 1983 was more than a homecoming. It was a pilgrimage to Jack Kerouac's origins as well. Antonelli was beginning work on a documentary about Kerouac's life, having received a research grant from the National Endowment for the Humanities. As he drove around his old haunts, he began to feel a real sense of destiny about the project. At the Edson cemetery, near his old high school, Antonelli inquired where Kerouac's grave was, though he felt strange visiting the tomb of someone he'd never met. When the gatekeeper handed him a simple map to the grave, he realized that there had been a caravan of believers before him who had traveled from all over the world to see the "sacred place, to sanctify Jack's memory."

Antonelli describes the moment:

Was that what I was up to? What will I do when I get there? Pray? I walked along feeling hypocritical but I kept going. The stone was a modest one. This didn't seem to have anything to do with my film. I was looking for ways to capture visually some of the mad excitement that Kerouac had captured in his writing. What could a flat tombstone sitting in a field of hundreds of other cookie-cutter graves have to do with that? I walked away, embarrassed that I ever went there, and took maybe four or five steps. Something in me was wrestling with the hipster that I had worked so hard to become, and the hipster was losing. I turned around and headed back to the stone and stopped and studied it. No sign really. . . . What could I say to a man who had been dead now for twenty years, even if his writing had helped to shape who I was even before I had ever read it?

I'd retraced his travels from Lowell to Colorado to Mexico to California, because they were the hip places to go in the sixties.

Everywhere I hitchhiked, I'd hear his name. Occasionally, I'd be asked, "You're from Lowell. What's it like in Kerouac's home-town?" Then I was the observer of an in-depth discussion with a group of Dharma Bums about the books that had sent them on a quest for some kind of spiritual Zen awakening in a world that had had its meaning squeezed out of it by racism, war, and capitalism. I knew all the values they were expounding on, but I didn't know they had came from Kerouac originally. From Lowell? How's that possible? How, in that cultural wasteland, could there have been a beacon of cool that had reached millions, and been at the root of both the Beats and the Hippies? I began to read Desolation Angels, The Subterranean, *the classic* On the Road, *and then the epic story of growing up in Lowell,* The Town and The City. *It was like reading my own story in parts. There were so many parallels to my life, only with a couple of decades separating us. I began to realize that most of my experimenting with drugs, sex, and rock 'n' roll had been done by Kerouac and his cronies so long before us that it made our adventures seem incredibly pale by comparison. Then I thought of making a film about him, figuring it must have been done already but, magically, it hadn't been.*

Now I was here, beginning to make the film, and I owed it all to him. I thanked him. I told him I'd do a good job. That was it. If I'd really thought about it, I would have asked him for his help, asked him to smile on the project, or, at least, not to get in the way. As it turned out, I didn't have to. He did anyway. But that's another story.

THE WAY OF THE ANCESTORS

People wonder about what you are pursuing.
You have to explain about the thread.
—William Stafford

For John Borton, pilgrimage into the past was galvanized by a deep personal need to make sense of his family. He describes himself going through a "frenzy of genealogy research" during which he uncovered a vast amount of old family photographs, letters, and other memorabilia. Within two years, he had journeyed to Texas, Wisconsin, and Michigan to interview his family. He was searching for answers to a nagging sense of pain and "not belonging—not being whole" that he shared with his two sisters and sought to understand.

> *Nana Borton's Field Family line took me to Boston where I traced her line back to 1650 in Boston. I finally located the Revolutionary War hero Lemuel Field, who really did fight at Bunker Hill. In his court document, now on microfiche in the National Archives, I found a summary of his whole war career, dictated in his own words. The phrases and word choices burst through time into my brain as I heard my grandmother's and my language echoed in his own. There was immediately a recognition through his words that this man was kin, flesh of my flesh, despite all the intervening centuries.*

> *Back to Michigan and California as I continued my search for the Borton ancestors, I found myself constantly overcoming parental voices in my head telling me this was a line I should not pursue. Yet I went on because I felt I could not live with failing to complete this journey to the end. My sisters offered moral support, but acknowledged they had experienced similar fear and could not have gone even this far.*

My youngest sister made a quilt of family photos printed on muslin and decorated with scraps of Nana Borton's fabrics and historic buttons. It boosted my spirits. My middle sister wrote me letters, did research, and helped me to make connections to important details in the letters and photos we had collected. She visited me and helped me organize the immense volume of materials into a more coherent whole and patterns began to emerge. I was once again able to ask the right questions. Then my father began to write to his relatives and pieces began to fall into place.

The strangest was when we received confirmation of a fact my middle sister and I had found in a Michigan courthouse that suggested our great-great-grandfather Borton had been adopted. Suddenly the sense we had felt all these years of something odd on this side of the family stood out in the light. This was why the census had shown no other listings, this was why the family had kept some sort of secret. Finally an aunt recalled the story she had heard about his being left with the Borton family during the Civil War while his mother went off to search for her husband and they never returned.

In his teens when he had been told, my great-great-grandfather, Fred Borton, was highly agitated and angry, feeling unloved and abandoned; adrift in the world. That feeling had been passed down from generation to generation for over a hundred years and seemed to be the emotion that had led my sisters and I to begin the search. Now we could heal ourselves and the family with the truth and begin to get on with our own lives. The haunting from the past could be put to rest. We knew who we were and could look to the future. My youngest sister now was able to have a

family and children. The rest of us breathed a great sigh of
release. The future is clear before us now that the past is in proper
focus. This journey has ended.

Borton's pilgrimage was as interior as it was exterior. As in any
great drama, finding the missing pieces of his world was a life-or-death
question. His search exemplifies the force that can well up from below,
from the soul, over a period of time, the desire to move toward the
wellspring that will rejuvenate us.

Photographer Eric Lawton's earliest memories are filled with his
mother's stories of her childhood in Tientsin, China. In 1988, he
realized his dream of journeying to China to find his family's home.
Before departing, his mother's childhood friend drew a map of the
street where their home had been, on what was then Woodrow
Wilson Road. After seventy-five years of wars and earthquakes,
Lawton didn't know if the house had withstood the ravages of time. He
brought a faded photograph of his grandfather, taken in 1920, on the
stone steps of the family home, a banister sweeping gracefully on either
side, a narrow wood tower rising above. In India, Lawton explains, the
confluence of rivers, the place where two rivers merge into one, is
called *sanghama*. His pilgrimage to China was his *sanghama*: to seek the
confluence of the river of his life's time with that of his ancestor.

I found the Hotel Astor, standing in time-worn dignity across
from the park where my mother played as a child. I looked to the
corner, where the house should have been. There was only a small
green garden. My heart stops. It was gone. A profound sense of
loss washes over me as I realize that my journey was in vain. I
sit on a wooden bench, where the house should be. It occurs to
me that the house must still be here. I feel anguish that I came
too late to touch it.

That night I phone home with heavy heart, and tell my mother that the house is gone. After a silence, she asks where I've searched. On hearing, she laughs and says: "No, the house wasn't across from Hotel Astor, it was down the road." I jump to my feet, ready to return at once, although it is midnight. At first light I hurry back with my interpreter. I find the oldest person on the street, an ancient chestnut vendor. We show him the map, asking if he can remember where these streets were. After an eternal moment, he points: my eyes follow his gnarled finger, and I see the stairs, the curved banister of my mother's home.

I run to the house, and, out of breath, I hold up my grandfather's picture. Seventy-five years melt away as I stand in the exact point of view of the photograph. On the stone steps sits a young Chinese boy, the same age as my mother when she lived here. We show him the photograph, tell him the story. He gets his father, who warmly invites us in. The room has high ceilings and a single window... a wooden floor, a bed at one end. I step out of this moment and float across the room, absorb the memory, inhale its latent presence, breathe it to life, and watch: How many times did my mother's hand run along this banister, worn from so many hands into this graceful form? What dreams were hinted at? Am I among those dreams? Did she dream of having me, her only child, at night while looking up at this ceiling? Sounds of footsteps approaching. An old woman's smiling face appears. She holds a time-worn album, its thick leather deeply resonant with hand-to-hand memory. We sit at a weathered table. She opens it, and the story of this house emerges: an earthquake took the spire, a war changed the front wall; it was an officers' quarters during an occupation. These people lived here once. Now five families share the house.

With their permission I photograph the house, the family, and especially the young boy, with whom I have found a wordless bond. They take my picture, as I stand where my grandfather stood in the faded photograph. I thank them, and it is time to go. As we walk down the stone steps, I turn and ask the father about the name of the street. It is no longer called Woodrow Wilson Road, he says. It is now called Liberation Way.

CONSIDERING THE MARVEL

Sometimes I go about in pity for myself, and all the while a great wind is bearing me across the sky.
—Ojibwa saying

In his book, *The Outermost House*, Henry Beston describes how when he was thirty-six years old, in 1927, he decided he needed to find "essentials." In the tradition of the Transcendentalists, he went into solitude on Cape Cod to see for himself the "elemental presences" that dwelled there and to witness the "incomparable pageant of nature and the year." Although he planned to stay only for short periods, once there he realized that he needed to "share its mysterious and elemental life." Ensconced, Beston in his book became a model witness for what nature has to teach us. There was always something "poetic and mysterious," such as the bird tracks in the sand dunes. One day, he contemplates the surf and looks out to sea, imagining what lies on the other side—Santiago de Compostela, "renown of pilgrims"—and recalling how when he was there he was offered a scallop shell, but "I would have none of it, and got myself a seashell from some Galician fisherfolk." This spirit of seeing for yourself and finding your own talismans reflects the true pilgrim spirit.

"Consider the marvel of what we see," he writes in the hushed tones of the contemplative traveler. "Somewhere in ocean, perhaps a thousand miles and more from this beach, the pulse beat of earth liberates a vibration, an ocean wave.... So it goes night and day, and will go till the secret heart of earth strikes out its last slow beat and the last wave dissolves upon the forsaken shore." During his stay, he notes how the length of the year is a "journey along a paper calendar" and that one must have "knowledge of the pilgrimage of the sun" to have a grasp of the wonder of the world.

Spending a year with Beston through his narrative helps us realize the range of pilgrimage available to us. He approached his journey to Cape Cod as the holiest of journeys; his reverence for the shrine he created there was as deep as the prophet's respect for ancestral shrines. The gift he brought back, his insights, his observations, are a constant reminder of the beauty and mystery available to those using, as the Sufis said, "the eyes of the heart." Like the greatest of travel writers, he reveals how any journey, whether as part of a crowd or in solitude, can produce the moment of awe, the vision, contact with the numinous. In stillness, at the still point of our journey, is the redemption of our wasted time.

Imagine what is behind the *presence* at these wisdom sites and places of pilgrimage. Imagine that its presence demands yours. The call that brought you here was a call to pay closer attention to the sacred source of your life. After all your preparation, the arduous journeying, the force that called you here is asking for something vital only you can give. What is it? What can you give back? Has your amazement been amazed yet?

Consider the marvel of your arrival.

THE TRAVELER'S LAMP

Never forget that your days are blessed. You may know how
to profit by them, or you may not, but they are blessed.
—Nadia Boulanger

For Basho, the lighting of the lamp each night of his journey was not only the means of illuminating his small room at the inn, but also the first step toward the sacred act of remembering.

"After lighting a lamp," he wrote of his visit to Sarashina Village, "I took out my pen and ink, and closed my eyes, trying to remember the sights I had seen and the poems I had composed during the day."

This is the practice of mindfulness. Basho ritualized each act on his journey; he realized there is no such thing as a throwaway gesture or a neutral thought. The very act of pilgrimage magnetizes each stage of the journey. So at the end of the day's arduous walk, he asked himself what he had seen, what he had felt.

How can we better illuminate our own experiences? In his book *American Places*, journalist William Zinsser recounts how he went searching for the "real" America in the late 1980s, a time when he was doubting if there was anything authentic left. He ventured to some of the noted places, including Yellowstone National Park; Kitty Hawk, site of the Wright Brother's first flight; and the Gettysburg Battle site where, he writes, "I was glad to be there as a pilgrim." His quest ended at Walden Pond.

The afternoon of his arrival, he sauntered over the grounds, contemplating the contribution of Thoreau to his own life. At the edge of the famous pond, he noticed a man whom he presumed to be from India, apparently in deep reverie. At an appropriate moment, Zinsser approached him and asked if he was indeed from India and, if so, why he had come so far. The man explained that he was a friend of Gandhi, who "always had planned to make a pilgrimage to Concord." Because of Gandhi's untimely death, the visitor had vowed to make it for him, to complete the pilgrimage and find out for himself what had given Thoreau the serenity to write the books that had inspired his friend to pursue the philosophy of civil disobedience.

Zinsser was very touched by the sentiment and the gesture of this man completing his friend's pilgrimage nearly forty years after Gandhi's death. There is great power in making a journey with a deep purpose, but any journey can be further deepened by seeking a broader perspective. If Zinsser had kept to himself, lost in his own private thoughts, he never would have seen Walden the same way.

On an ordinary journey, one designed for sheer entertainment, diversion, or self-reward for a year of hard work, there would be no obvious need to go out of your way to strike up a conversation with a perfect stranger.

But a pilgrimage asks us to do exactly that. The path needs more light. To shine the light of your own natural curiosity into the world of another traveler can reveal wonders. To remember the mysteries you forgot at home.

THE WINDY WALLS OF TROY

No man is greater than his destiny.
—Homer, *Iliad*

In 1993, I made the pilgrimage to Troy. For the wind of it, for the sound of it, for the feeling in the soles of my feet of touching the ground I'd read about since boyhood. The land of Helen, whose passion for Paris inspired the "ten thousand ships" to rescue her. The land of Homer.

Alexander the Great had paid homage to the reputed grave of Achilles on his way to India, and Mark Twain stopped here on his Holy Land pilgrimage. Now I was leading a group to the site, which I was

The fabled Scaean Gates of Troy, built around 1250 B.C.E., through which was pulled, Homer tells us, the fateful Trojan Horse. On the left are the foundation stones of the Great Tower, from which King Priam watched Achilles do battle with Hector.

aware could easily disappoint those who had only bad watercolor paintings from old schoolbooks with which to imagine the citadel that withstood the Greek army of Agamemnon and Odysseus for nine long years. I knew I could regale my group with the history of the famous archaeological digs, from Heinrich Schliemann to the recent teams from the University of Cincinnati. But I sensed I'd need more to rouse the power of the place, so before leaving the States I found a scene from Homer's *Iliad* and six different translations of it, from Alexander Pope to Richard Lattimore.

When we arrived at Hissarlik, the group grew quiet as we approached the Scaean Gates. I explained that the old cobbles were the remnant of the rampway that the Trojan Horse rolled over into the besieged city. Threading our way through the ruins, I pointed out the place where the so-called Mask of Agamemnon was discovered, the marble seats of an old theater, a few pediments from a temple to Athena.

Then, sitting on a bluff overlooking the fields where the great war took place, I handed out photocopies of the heartbreaking scene from the *Iliad* in which the Trojan hero, Hector, says good-bye to his wife and two-year-old son on the embattlements of the besieged citadel. One by one, the tour participants read Homer's glorious verses, each version reflecting the different ways in which the generations look at war, heroism, and the gods. Each reading touched a part of us that wouldn't have been reached had we not had the words to make the mute stones all around us speak.

There, in the falling light of day, the wind in my hair, I read and felt my soul rising, recalling Homer's "winged words."

I am constantly looking for methods to help myself and others see the magic of a place, feel the magic performed by the saint or artist or hero we have come so far to engage.

The gardens at Giverny are a supreme example of the pilgrimage brought home, made permanent, infused as a way of life. How this came to be is hinted at by author Guy de Maupassant, who described accompanying his friend Claude Monet "on his quest for impressions. At such times he was no longer a painter but a hunter. . . ." In his preface for the catalog of the Monet-Rodin exhibition of 1889, poet Octave Mirbeau wrote that Monet "observed that on an average day, a given effect hardly lasts thirty minutes. Hence he had to tell the story of those thirty minutes, which is to say that in a given piece of nature, those minutes express both harmony in light, and harmony in concordant movements. . . ."

This is to say that light itself was a shrine to Monet, what he sought when he journeyed to the cathedral at Rheims, the train station in Paris, the haystacks in Provence. Not simply the site, but the *sight*, the sight of light.

So genuinely moved was he by the miracle of light at play in the fields, it became his passion to discover, on a daily basis, "the life contained in things."

Alexander Eliot, former art critic for *Time* magazine, describes his own rituals when traveling: "When I am back from the day, I try to go over it, try to honor it before going asleep. For years I have made the point of memorizing paintings at museums. I always tell people to *simplify* their museum experience. Find one painter, or just a few paintings, and pay attention to *those*. If a work of art excites you, memorize it *with your eyes and your imagination* right there in the museum and you will have it forever. You can be a collector that way! If, on some enchanted evening, you see a piece of sculpture or a painting, you grab on to it, latch on to it. You don't gorge on the food at a great meal. You should taste the food, not shovel it down. It's the same with traveling."

Imagine following light for an entire day. Try to see the way a painter would, the play light makes on buildings, the way architectural details call forth the play of shadows over the course of a day. Think of the different ways light affects you, and in its absence, the dark.

THE TRAVELER'S TASKS

There are no days in life so memorable as those
which vibrated to some stroke of the imagination.
—Ralph Waldo Emerson

O nce you arrive at your destination, find your inn for the night and set your baggage down. Open your traveler's satchel and take out your notebook and map. Unless you are feeling shattered or ill, try not to rest too soon, as it can throw your rhythm off for several days. Instead, take a brief walk. This is a way of immediately acclimating yourself. It allows time for your "soul to catch up." It helps you get your bearings and alleviates the restlessness often experienced by travelers when they try to sleep without knowing where they are.

Walk and stay out until your normal sleeping time. While walking, renew your vow to make this journey a pilgrimage that is sacred to *you*. Recall why you made the trip in the first place. Very often, the great dragons of doubt set in, snarling nasty thoughts about the money spent, the time taken off, the undone deeds at home. The great nomad Bruce Chatwin often asked himself when he arrived at an unfamiliar place, *What am I doing here?* As a pilgrim, you want to ask that of yourself, then recount, recapitulate your answer in your journal, on a postcard, or in a prayer in a favorite church.

For me, arrival also means bringing out the touchstone. In a new place, the testing begins with finding the center, whether it's a tiny Mediterranean fishing village or a busy city in Spain. My first task is always to walk toward the center of town, as if I am in a labyrinth, and it usually turns out to be an old café, a taverna, a pub, an outdoor

Long thought to be huts for shepherds, cláchains or "beehive huts," such as this ninth- or tenth-century one on Inishmore in the Aran Islands, Ireland, are now believed to have functioned as "pilgrim hostels."

restaurant, the steps of a library, a bench in front of a bookstore. I need to feel the ripple of conversation, the joy of laughter, the whirlwind of ideas, to know I have arrived. A walk along the promenade if you are in a Latin country can accomplish this.

The essential task is to feel the thrill of completing your pilgrimage. If we remember that the word *thrill* originally referred to the vibrations the arrow made when it hits the target, than the pleasure is compounded. There is joy in having arrived, moment by moment.

"The purpose is to be in the present moment and enjoy each step you make," says Buddhist monk Thich Nhat Hanh. "Therefore you have to shake off all worries and anxieties, not thinking of the future, not thinking of the past, just enjoying the present moment." Greeting others soulfully and respectfully, "in whatever form you use, the Buddha is present.... Suddenly, the Buddha in each of us begins to shine, and we are in touch with the present moment."

A woodblock print of a public fountain and gathering place in eighteenth-century Lisbon, Portugal.

To stay true to this practice, to stay focused on the purpose for your journey, recall each morning before you leave your room the gentle advice of the explorer who learned after meandering the world that you must *pass by whatever you do not love.*

At twilight the first night of my visit to Marrakech, Morocco, I resisted the temptation to stay inside my hotel and eat dinner and then crash, despite immense weariness and even leeriness of a strange new place. Instead, I stepped outside into the charivari of smells and sounds in the market square.

Minutes later, I paused near a group of musicians and storytellers who were setting up their drums amid the hurly-burly of marketers. One of them drew a circle in the dirt around himself, and invited those of us lingering to step inside through a small opening he had left.

Once we were inside the magic circle, he closed it up and began to play music. When night set, he transformed into a magician storyteller, ignoring everyone outside the circle. Singers, drummers, dancers, magicians came and went, trailing joy in the warm desert air.

Nine hours later, he allowed us to leave. I wandered back to my hotel, feeling like I could fly home after only one evening. I felt preternaturally alive, my ears ringing with the desert drumming. I felt sated, sure that I didn't have to travel any farther, that I was already where I needed to be. How much happier could I be?

THE OFFERING

God wants the heart.
—The Talmud

At Troy, I felt the need to honor the gods of the site. Those divinities who have blessed us with a journey await our offerings at every sacred destination, whether in the form of a prayer, a bow, a kneeling to the ground, or a recitation from a sacred text. In Bali, food is left at the temples; in Ireland, strips of cloth are left hanging on nearby trees and money is donated to priests; in Tibet, pilgrims might leave behind a gift of yak butter to the monastery they are visiting. Always an offering, a sanctifying.

There are a multitude of ways you can cultivate a sense of gratitude. Your journey is the result your effort in conjunction with countless others. In Bali, the ritual gift is an offering of flowers or fruit. To walk down the streets of Denpasar, or any small village, is to witness

A monk divines the meaning of I Ching yarrow sticks he has thrown on behalf of a young pilgrim on the terrace of the Bayon, Angkor Thom, Cambodia.

an endless parade of people walking to and from temples with gifts for the gods. Leaving a small donation is another common ritual. A few coins in a poorbox is a way not only of helping, but of saying thank you for the gift you've been given by having arrived safely. I think of the white flowers at the home of Mary in Ephesus, Turkey; the wine bottles and candles in front of the John Lennon shrine in Prague; white ribbons in the holly bushes around the Chalice Well in Glastonbury, England.

A small token of appreciation is in order even for a pilgrimage to a literary shrine. Poet Tess Gallagher tells me the gravesite of her husband, writer Raymond Carver, has become a literary shrine. Every time she visits the site outside of Port Townsend, Washington, she finds gifts of flowers or poems.

Imagine what the equivalents of a gracious arrival are for you. On the evening of your arrival, read from a sacred text that was written on the holy ground you stand upon. Write down something you want your grandchildren to remember you by. Leave behind an offering. Let your joy show. Savor the moment. Linger a while. Relish the idea that for now you are no longer a stranger in this world. Wonder about the saving grace that came your way. Remember that sacred places are those that eternity shines through, like sunlight through a rose window.

A graffiti image of John Lennon transformed into a popular shrine, complete with offerings of incense and candles, near the Charles Bridge, Prague, Czech Republic.

In summer 1984, I co-led a literary tour to Ireland with storyteller Gioia Timpanelli and poet Robert Bly. We experienced marvelous sights and sounds as we spiraled around the country, but the most memorable turned out to be sheer serendipity. On the final night of the tour, we returned to Dublin, where Bly startled us with the news that he had convinced Irish poet Seamus Heaney to travel down from Belfast and join us at the Shelbourne Hotel for a reading.

*At a café near the cathedral in Bath, England, vet-
eran traveler Trevor Green, of Sheffield, England,
spends a languorous afternoon writing letters, making
entries in his journal, and sketching.*

What followed was an evening's revival of the old Celtic bardic
duels, conducted in good fun. I recall Bly beaming with pride as he
introduced Heaney, saying, "Seamus, give us some Yeats." Heaney
crossed his legs, smiled, then recited poem after poem from memory.

Turning back to Bly, he challenged the American to follow him up, but only with poems learned by heart. Bly complied with poems by Rilke and Akmatova.

I recently found some verses I wrote that evening, stuck for the last fourteen years in a small volume of Yeat's selected poetry. In a heartbeat, I was transported back to a land I love by these simple images of Heaney:

> He runs his long fingers through his shock of white hair,
> his gaze racing out to the old stone house in Sligo,
> as he rouses the presence of Yeats,
> his second father.

> He sits still on his seat, as if on the stone ledge
> of the Aran Islands, held fast by the wind,
> rooted in ancient rock,
> a pilgrim contemplating

> how strange and marvelous things
> come to the one who journeys to
> the wishing chair made
> of salty old seastones.

VII

BRINGING BACK
THE BOON

How long the road is. But, for all the time
the journey has already taken, how you have needed
every second of it in order to learn what
the road passes by.

—Dag Hammarskjöld, *Markings*

ONCE UPON A TIME," THE OLD GREENLANDER told Danish explorer Knut Rasmussen, "there was a man who lived farther north than any of the settlements. He hunted bears every spring on a dogsledge.

"Once, during the chase, he came upon strange sledge-tracks and made up his mind to seek out the people who had made them. So he set out on his bear-hunts the next year earlier than he was wont to do. The third day, he came to houses different in appearance from those to which he was accustomed. But they met with no people; fresh tracks, though, showed that the settlement had been only recently left.

"When the bear-hunter drove off the following year, he took wood with him, as a gift to the strangers; for he thought they must suffer greatly from the want of wood, as they used narwhals' tusks for the roof-beams of their houses.

"But he did not meet with the strangers on his second visit either. True, the tracks were newer than they had been the last time, but he did not dare to follow them up, and thus put a still greater distance between himself and his own village. He contented himself with burying the wood he had brought with him in the snow near the houses, and then, having presented his gifts, he went home.

"The third year he raised the best team of dogs that he had ever had and, earlier than was his custom, he drove north after bears and the strange people. When at last he reached the village, it was just as it had been the other years; the inhabitants had gone; but in the snow, where he had left his wood, they had hidden a large bundle of walrus tusks and inside, in the entrance passage, lay a magnificent bitch and puppies. These were the return gifts of the strangers.

"He put them on his sledge and drove back home; but the people who lived north of all other men he never found."

This tantalizing legend of "sledge tracks northward" is a worthy parable for travelers everywhere. We are in mythic territory, hearing a wisdom tale from an unexpected source. The beauty of the tale is that it encourages us to ask who it is that has been bestowing gifts upon us on our own journeys, then suggests that it is all right if we never find out if it is a matter of fate, destiny, the gods, or the "strangers to the north."

Some may cringe at the ending to the hunter's story. How can he turn away, not knowing the source of the gift? But the old Greenlander concluded that "Beyond all that is mystery."

Imagine your return journey as the last act of an epic story. Which moments gleamed brighter, gave you pause, challenged all your previous beliefs, reconfirmed your belief in the power at the center? How did you happen upon them? Were they self-willed, the result of punctilious planning, or were they serendipitous? Did you feel any strange visitations of joy? Can you recapture them now that you are home?

Epiphanies sometimes flash and flare for pilgrims, but there are also flickering moments of discovery on your journey, seen out of the corner of your eye. Small joys, humble experiences, such as twilight falling on the old columns of Amiens cathedral while the choir practiced; the tumble of dominoes and tinkle of children's laughter in the cafés next to the Blue Mosque; the woman who dashed across the street in a pummeling rain to give you directions to poet Anna Akmatova's apartment in St. Petersburg, after you had walked in circles for three hours, utterly lost.

You knew these things about people and places before you left

*According to popular belief, the function of the needlepoint
minaret towers, such as these of the Blue Mosque in
Istanbul, Turkey, is to pierce the sky so that the prayers of
the faithful can rise more easily into heaven.*

home, but you had forgotten them. This journey reminded you of the
sacred rhythms. How will you remember to remember when you
return home?

The Chinese master Qingyuan Weixin described the living paradox that threads through soulful travel stories. When the scales of laziness fall over our eyes and we have begun to take life for granted, we must take an arduous journey to relearn the essential truths of the life right before our eyes.

> *When I had not yet begun to study Zen thirty years ago, I thought*
> *that mountains are mountains and waters are waters. Later when*
> *I studied personally with my master, I entered realization and*
> *understood that mountains are not mountains, waters are not*
> *waters. Now that I abide in the way of no-seeking, I see as before*
> *that mountains are just mountains, waters are just waters.*

René Daumal's stirring parable *Mount Analogue* is an unfinished tale about an adventure on a yacht named *Impossible* to a mysterious island featuring a legendary mountain. The questing souls are guided up the mountain by the mysterious powers of the islanders, learning the undersong of meaning as they ascend. Like Marcel Proust, they are seeking "the privileged moment," the epiphany of a revelation, yet are perplexed to learn how difficult it is to begin, even just to set up camp, much less ascend a mountain. There are obstacles everywhere. As Daumal writes, "To return to the source, one must travel in the opposite direction."

Daumal's characters were not content with mere book-learning. Like all pilgrims of the spirit, they needed to move beyond merely reading about the legendary mountain and actually set foot on it. Glory and the heroism of the ascent to the summit are not the point of the story. Interwoven into the tale is the understanding that the ascent is not complete without the descent. Near the end of the story is a gold-threaded detail we might call "The Pilgrim's Law":

> *A soulful traveler replenishes the camp before moving on for those*

*who will follow, and you must share whatever wisdom you've
been blessed with on your journey with those who are about to set
out on their own journey.*

Daumal's parable touches on another sacred element of the journey
with deep purpose: the need to reflect upon its meaning, then return
home and remember to live with redoubled courage.

*In the process of putting so much pressure on language, thought
ceases to be satisfied with the support of words; it bursts away
from them in order to seek its resolution elsewhere. This "elsewhere" should not be understood as a transcendent realm, a mysterious metaphysical domain.*

*This "elsewhere" is "here" in the immediacy of real life. It is from
right here that our thoughts rise up, and it is here that they must
come back. But after what travels! Live first; then turn to philosophy; but in the third place, live again. Then man in Plato's cave
has to go out and contemplate the light of the sun; then, strength-
ened by this light, which he keeps in his memory, he has to return
to the cave. Verbal philosophy is only a necessary stage in this
voyage.*

After our great round of travels, through time and space, art and literature, religious quests and nature exploration, here is the undersong
of pilgrimage. As Fyodor Dostoyevski wrote, "Thou shall love life more
than the meaning of life."

Like the climbers of Mount Analogue, the pilgrim feels a different
call and is changed by the journey. The deepest of those changes is the
need to share the gold, the wisdom, the boon of the journey. But the
bitter truth about coming home from a long journey is that we soon
learn that one man's mystery can be another man's superstition. How
do we describe the ineffable?

It is said in Venice that upon their return, Marco Polo and his father were not even recognized because of their tattered traveler's rags. But inside their tattered clothes were sewn diamonds and jewels from their far-flung journeys. Were they simply to be traded for profit, or were they physical proof of their literally unbelievable travels, in case they were not believed?

Our "diamonds and jewels" are not our real diamonds and jewels. Boasting, bragging, and brandishing is guaranteed to garner hostility.

In Joseph Campbell's popular book of essays *Myths to Live By*, he described something pertinent to our theme of sacred journeys: "The ultimate aim of the quest, if one is to return, must be neither release nor ecstasy for oneself, but the wisdom and the power to serve others."

Now I can't hear a travel story, watch a film, or read a book without asking, "What was brought home? Where is the *gift?* Show me the jewels sewn in the lining of your coat. Where is the boon?"

The ancient wisdom teachers taught that the ultimate answer to the sorrows of the world is the boon of increased self-knowledge. Anthropologist Lewis Hyde's idea from his book *The Gift* is that in ancient times a true gift was "the agent of change." A person dare not hold on too long to one, because it would be the equivalent of the hoary old dragon "hoarding the gold."

In his essay "A Witness for Poetry," Oregon poet William Stafford describes giving a lecture once, dreading that he would be treated like a relic, asked things like, "How was it back in 1948?"

Instead, he was asked about a subject dear to his heart—the process by which he wrote poetry. "It's strange," he ends the essay, "to think that there might be things that we know that people [who] live one hundred years from now would like to know. We forget to say them."

That insight is a boon to poets and travelers everywhere. This is the key to the poetry of pilgrimage: The story that we bring back from our journeys *is* the boon. It is the gift of grace that was passed to us in the heart of our journey. Perhaps it was in the form of an insight into our spiritual life, a glimpse of the wisdom traditions of a radically different culture, a shiver of compassion, an increment of knowledge. All these must now be passed on. The boon—at Delphi, at Elephanta, at Angkor, at a local shrine, at your father's gravesite, at the hospital where you were born—is a presence in the soul of the world that can be sensed and honored and carried home in your heart.

Imagine any resistance or disbelief or jealousy you may encounter when you return home as personified in the threshold guardian.

A snake-charmer and storyteller regales the crowd in the old market square of Djemaa el Fna, Marrakesh, Morocco.

Custom requires that you make some kind of peace offering to the guardian at the threshold of your homeland.

To reimagine your journey again and again as you return home can be solace for the pain of crossing the final threshold. The family and friends who feted you when you departed may be busy with their own lives and mysteriously disappear when you call to share your travel stories, slides, and astonishments.

Prepare yourself. It will be harder than you think to find an audience for your stories. If you get a chance, express gratitudes rather than platitudes when you get home. The real jewels are the hidden treasure-stories many people at home, everywhere throughout time, have longed to hear—stories of the real Shangri-la, tales of what the soul, not the ego, endured.

Tell what you have learned from your journey.

The oldest and soundest of all boons is hard-earned wisdom.

FOR THE MARVELS

*I am certain of nothing but the holiness of the heart's affections
and the truth of imagination—what the imagination seizes as
beauty must be truth—whether it existed before or not.*
—John Keats, 1817

I am thrilled each time I reread the conclusion of the twelfth-century guidebook *The Marvels of Rome*. This book was the first of its kind to move beyond the fervid relic-hunting of the day to lead the pilgrim and traveler to the wonders of ancient architecture and history. The first sense that there may be something worthwhile to remember from the past, the creations of ordinary people, is hinted at in these lovely lines:

> *These and more temples and palaces of emperors, consuls, sena-
> tors and prefects were inside this Roman city in the time of the
> heathen, as we have read in the old chronicles, have seen with
> our own eyes, and have heard the ancient men tell of. In writing
> we have tried as well as we could to bring back to the human
> memory how great was their beauty in gold, silver, brass, ivory
> and ancient stones.*

In this way, the art of remembering, the skill with which to "bring back to the human memory how great was their beauty," we continually reconstruct our own lives. Recollection is the final discipline of the pilgrim-poet-traveler, which entails recalling the vows taken before departing, revering the idea that once we have been blessed with the gift of the journey, so now we must bless. We can continually recall beauty through the practice of memory, through daily acts of imagination that seize the moments that once seized our hearts.

And the strange thing is, once you do, you may find, as Carl Sandburg did, that

> *When nothing is ahead of you, then you have come to an end.*
> *Where nothing is behind you, then ahead of you is a beginning.*

BACK TO THE BEGINNING

It is a strange thing to come home. While yet on the journey,
you cannot at all realize how strange it will be.
—Selma Lagerlöf (1858–1940)

For Trish O'Rielly, coming home means letting go for awhile of the travels so an opening can be created. She needs time to evaluate what was endured. "That part never ends, hopefully!" she laughs. "It is strange and difficult, of course, because your world at home is calling to you. But you have to honor your memory first. I think of the task as 'reestablishing the *beginning point*,' because you are now back where you started and you have to know now you've come full circle. I feel strongly about the new beginning, the continuum, the next step. If we don't know where we've been, how do we know what to do the next time?"

Taking time when you return home, she believes, helps the process, allows the model to unfold again. Otherwise, as many travelers discover to their dismay, one journey starts to blur with the next, and anxiety may begin to overwhelm the desire to take the next pilgrimage.

Michael Guillén is fond of the ancient Mayan custom of the bachelor pilgrimage to the sea, in which young men bring shells, fruit, and stones back from their journeys to decorate the altars at home, as symbols of fertility. It has inspired a personal ritual of creating altars out of his pilgrimages, and Guillen recommends the exercise for others.

"Bring home an aspect from every journey for your altar at home," he says. "Make it part of your altar at home. What's important to me is this is the domestic part of Latino life; our altars protect our home. So bring something home to re-create the altar—a smooth mineral, a touchstone. This is an important part of pilgrimage, the recreating of *memory rituals* to help remember people you lost. Another way for me is to remember others and to remember myself *honestly.*"

On the wall of a café located in the shadows of the Acropolis in Athens hangs a wooden "memory box," or assemblage of sculptural details, that the café owner has collected from nearby ruins and his travels around Greece—an imaginative example of what any pilgrim can create upon their return.

For Joan Marler, the boon means the gratitude we have even for the ordeals that arose on the pilgrimage. She calls these transformations "gift moments," and to realize them awakens the "story of the journey." Her most dramatic example is the closing ritual she designed for a tour she led to the island of Malta, where the group spent four hours in an ancient temple. The time itself was the gift, as local authorities had closed the temple after dark to visitors because of recent vandalism by local hunters. "It was a very special time, twilight, darkness, stars and moon, candles, ceremony on an island that was once entirely sacred."

Like most of us, Joan faces the same dilemma when she comes home: "How do we keep sacred memories alive? How to make the journey part of our lives once we are back in the daily grind? I see the time of return as reintegration time, a time to recall as much as possible about the trip, a time of listening to dreams and creating something new *so the awakening continues.* This is so important because you've changed. Something shifted and came to consciousness. Now you know the sacred is everywhere. Now you know the miniature is inside you. And once again, the storytelling allows things to 'come up,' trust your own wisdom. We must remember this: The journey is a miniature of the bigger one which is life. It contains all of it. You found the essence if you can find the gift moment that has all of it inside."

For Pohsuan Zaide, a therapist in Vancouver, British Columbia, the central challenge of her travels is learning to honor them by paying finer attention to her life when she returns home. "My travels through the Mediterranean a few years ago," she recollects, "kept me alive during a difficult period. If I lose track of that, my life becomes excruciating." She says that what her pilgrimage to such places as Epidauras in Greece and Ephesus in Turkey accomplished for her is that they confirmed that it's not enough to live on the surface of life.

"The secret that the ancient Greeks knew is that it's all here and now, and there's creativity all around me to keep me alive, if I look for

Michigan artist, Mary Rezmerski's, collage in memory of her pilgrimage to the Mediterranean is a soulful example of how travelers can keep their journeys alive—and inspire new ones.

it. There were moments on the tour, such as one under an olive tree on the island of Paros, that were like glitterings that helped open deep places in me and made me yearn for more creativity in my life when I

"Time and the Typewriter," a window display in a Paris stationery store. An ordinary example of an extraordinary visual parable for honoring time by writing about it.

got home. That was my life lesson from the ancient Greeks: that I can get through Dante's hell if I can recall the magic of my pilgrimage, and that is possible to create a pilgrim life for myself *here*, a deeply felt, fully breathed life. I can see now that a true pilgrimage, if it's to Epidaurus or to a clinic in the inner city, is a way to bring you closer to God. They are both the center of the world. Now I know that British Columbia can also be seen as the heart of the world, like Henry Miller said about Epidaurus. We're all meaning-seeking creatures; sometimes it take a journey to remind us of that."

Imagine being a pilgrim to the Temple of Time on the Via Borgia in medieval Rome. The ornate building housed and displayed the clockworks marking out public time. No one had ever witnessed the ticktock progression before; the sight of time disappearing before their eyes fascinated and terrified the pilgrims, who lined up for miles to witness the spectacle. A returning modern traveler may consider time to be likewise alternately fascinating and terrifying.

How can we capture time when we come home? Complete your travel journal. Finalize your sketches. Create an original style of photograph album that enshrines your journey your way. A friend of mine makes collages from photographs, newspaper clippings, even leaves and pine needles gathered from her journeys. Another woman I know assembles talismans, such as stones, leaves, and old postcards, into what she calls "memory boxes" that she hangs on her wall as a permanent reminder of each of her travels. Several friends have revived the tradition of altars.

What do you think John Bunyan meant when he wrote at the end of *Pilgrim's Progress:*

> *Old things are past away, all's become new.*
> *Strange! he's another man, upon my word. . . .*

Ask yourself if you feel like you are a different person. If so, in what ways? Do the roads around your home seem altered, the food taste different, your everyday thoughts influenced by what you encountered on your pilgrimage? Much may seem changed, but the challenge now is to use the insights gathered on the road to see your everyday life as a pilgrimage. In ways like these, as Thich Nhat Hanh writes, "The path around our home is also the ground of awakening."

Remember again and again that the true pilgrimage is into the undiscovered land of your own imagination, which you could not have explored any other way than through these lands, with gratitude in your satchel and the compassion for all you see as your touchstone.

Recall the voice that spoke to Tolstoy in a dream at the end of his life: "See that you remember." It is a line that would look good stamped into our passports.

CELEBRATE ME HOME

If a man set out from home on a journey, and
kept right on going, he would come
back to his own front door.
—Sir John Mandeville, fourteenth century

Our old world will appear changed and strangified in proportion to how much we changed on our journey. If indeed it was a soulful journey, our former life may be nearly unrecognizable. Old friends may be genuinely interested in the tale-telling and not just the clichés of the journey, or they may react with envy, jealousy, or resentment.

Above all, *celebrate* your pilgrimage with a ritual feast. Bring family and friends together to ceremoniously mark the time and the passage. Sacred meals are a way to show gratitude and express joy, which are hallmarks of the well-lived life and the soulfully completed journey.

"True pilgrimage changes lives," says Martin Palmer in *Sacred Journeys*, "whether we go halfway around the world or out to our own backyards." What matters is whether we go *in* as we go out. Naturalist John Muir evoked the heart of the pilgrimage in his description of a single day's hike through a grand wilderness: "I only went out for a walk, and finally concluded to stay out till sundown, for going out, I found was really going in."

The challenge is to learn how to carry over the quality of the journey into your everyday life. The art of pilgrimage is the craft of taking time seriously, elegantly. What every traveler confronts sooner or later is that the way we spend each day of our travel ... is the way we spend our lives. Inspired by our journey, perhaps we can learn the "true life" we were searching for is *here*, where our travels and our home life overlap.

For only then shall we know that the end of our explorations, as T. S. Eliot wrote,

> *will be to arrive where we started*
> *and know the place for the first time.*

WALK ON, WALK ON

> *Ask what is in the wind*
> *ask what is sacred.*
> —Margaret Atwood

In the winter of 1975 I was invited by Steve Birkett, a friend I had worked with in the avocado groves of a kibbutz in Israel, to spend Christmas with his family at their home in the village of Liversedge, Yorkshire, in the north of England. On the first day, Steve took me on a bracing hike through the heathered downs, and on the second day to a soccer match at the stadium in nearby Leeds. All these years later, I don't recall who won, who scored, or what the weather was like. What I've never forgotten is the end of the match. Sixty thousand football fans set down their pints and programs, linked arms, and sang their club song, "You'll Never Walk Alone." I was stunned at the choice of an old Broadway song, overwhelmed by the display of public passion, and surprised by own emotional response as I joined in.

A traveler sauntering home to the village of Patcham, near Brighton, England.

After dinner, Steve was my guide on a classic pub crawl to a number of vintage country pubs, ending up at a remote sixteenth-century pub somewhere in the fogbound moors. At precisely ten minutes to eleven, closing time all across the land, the locals set down their pint glasses. Once again, they linked arms to sing in unison the club song. Somehow, out there on the moors, it sounded different, an echo from ancient times when a stranger was something to be reckoned with. On one side of the door, the stranger was somebody to be suspected; on the other, someone in need of warmth, food, and drink, a friend, a story for the night.

If you have ever threaded the darkest labyrinth of doubt, despair, and loneliness in the middle of the pilgrimage, with an attitude of gratitude for and solidarity with the travelers who have gone before, you too might know the bewildering ecstasy, the "thump and lift of the heart" I felt that night.

It's for moments like this that you left home—to no longer feel like a stranger in the world, to test your mettle against the strength of the fates, to find the unmet friends, and hear that no matter how far you wander as a pilgrim, "You'll Never Walk Alone."

PILGRIMS TO ANGKOR, TURN RIGHT

—A sign for travelers outside the Angkor complex, 1920s

On our last day at Angkor, my brother and I wandered down the old road beyond the vine-strangled stones if the Ta Prohm temple. Along the roadway was the recently discovered Pilgrim's Hostel. In my small, crude guidebook, purchased for fifty cents from

The Pilgrim's Hostel, Angkor Wat, Cambodia.

a one-armed vendor near the entrance, I read that the main temples had been rediscovered by French explorers in the 1840s, but this simple building lay undetected a mere few yards from the road until 1994. For centuries, pilgrims had stayed there after walking hundreds of miles from all over Southeast Asia to see heaven on earth, a paradise of stone and water and sanctuaries filled with 10,000 statues of the Buddha. The pilgrims chanced brigands and dacoits, dangerous animals and illness, but their imaginations had been inspired by faith. They had a purpose. I felt a remarkable kinship with them.

All my adult life, I had been enchanted by this dream of ruins, as if living out that single image from the book my father gave me for reasons I'll never know. I felt inconsolably lonely until I recalled the old hunter from Greenland who had the grace to simply accept the gift from the far north and receive the beauty of the mystery.

Late that afternoon, while deep in the dank corridors of the haunting temple of Bayon, with its fifty-four colossal faces of the Bodhisattva Avalokiteshvara staring at me with their enigmatic smiles, I thought of my last conversation with my father. He asked me what I had assumed to be obvious to him: "Did my love of books influence you?"

The words burned like a branding iron as I lit a candle and sticks of incense for him and, in the Bayon's dark corridors, said a silent prayer that his spirit might find peace.

Twilight was coming on. My brother and I dashed back to Angkor Wat and climbed the precipitously steep steps to the highest terrace to watch the sunset over the distant treetops of the jungle. Designed to make the pilgrim conscious of an ascent to a higher level, not just of altitude but consciousness, the stairs were worn to a deep groove by ten centuries of footsteps. Only at the top could we finally rest.

Sitting there, sweating profusely in the jungle heat, monks to the left and monks to the right, I thought of that beautiful line by Albert Camus, who wrote that a man's life is nothing more than the

My brother Paul Cousineau pauses on the steep ascent to the main sanctuary at Angkor Wat to contemplate the time-worn steps behind him.

rediscovery, through the detours of art, of those one or two images that first opened his heart.

How was it, I wondered, that I was moved so completely by this place? I was deeply sympathetic to Buddhist and Hindu beliefs, but did not practice. I was an avid reader of archaeology, but had only a rudimentary knowledge of Southeast Asian art. And yet I felt, in ways that defy category, as though I had come home.

The fiery sun dropped quickly beneath the horizon. The night came on, swarming with insects and strange sounds from the surrounding forest. In the shadows of the nearby villages, gas lamps flickered on. One by one, the monks and a handful of travelers began the precipitous descent down the hundreds of steps to the long causeway and a mile beyond to the perimeter road.

I leaned against the time-burnished stone pillars and gazed silently at the setting sun. In our familiar way, my brother and I simply nodded to each other, smiled, each knowing that the other was thinking of our father.

Before I began the descent, I happened to notice a single thin flame of light from a votive candle far down the corridor in the Hall of Buddhas. At each of the four levels of the descent, I looked back and up, and by a miracle of architecture, the thin flame was still visible. Not unlike the flame of my father's spirit in me, I thought, as I simultaneously looked back over my life and saw the thin, barely discernable light of his love, still there, still flickering, lending faith and direction to my path.

Knowing this, something in me felt completed. Only though a journey such as this could I come full circle in my life and touch something sacred that could revitalize my life.

Walking in the thick darkness of the Cambodian night, my sandals slapping against the ancient stones of the long causeway, a thought, wedged in from some distant time, arose in my mind. *Maybe we die twice. Once when our heart stops. Again when the living stop telling stories about us.*

In that moment, my heart rumbled with joy. My pilgrimage was complete, the journey with my father had ended. Another began the moment I turned away from the tiny flicker of red light and saw nothing but darkness in the forest surrounding the ancient temple and heard nothing but the sound of a single bell ringing from a distant temple.

The gift was at hand.

May the stars light your way
and may you find the interior road.
Forward!
—traditional Irish farewell

GRATITUDES

FOR LENDING GUIDANCE TO THIS WAYWARD TRAVELER, I would like to express my gratitude to the following band of pilgrims who shared their wisdom about pilgrimage: Huston Smith, Jay Fikes, Alan Jones, Alexander Eliot, Lauren Artress, Gary Rhine, Mort Rosenblum, Anthony Lawlor, John Nance, Ed Bernbaum, and Robert A. Johnson. I am also grateful to Goody Cable, Haydn Reiss, David Darling, Joan Marler, Trish O'Rielly, Bob Cooper, James Van Harper, John Borton, Valerie Andrews, and Eric Lawton for their advice on travel-related matters, including personal stories, reading lists, warnings, road remedies, and friendship. Also up for a cup of gratitude is Steve at Café Greco in North Beach for his ambrosial cappuccinos on my errant journeys. Thanks to Gail Evenari for permission to quote from the transcript of *The Wayfarers*, and to Jeannette Hermann for her spirited gifts of ambience on our art and literary tours, Michael Guillén for his soulful guiding through Guatemala, and Raymond and Louise Guy of Sudbury, Ontario, for the invitation to participate in our family's memorial canoe trip in 1995. A hearty *labas* to Sarunas Marciulionis for his generous hospitality in Vilnius, and a resounding *merci* to Jean-François Pasquilini for his most recent gracious hospitality in Paris, where early drafts of this work were written.

Many thanks also to all of the pilgrim guides at Conari Press: my publishers Will Glennon and Mary Jane Ryan, the indefatigable Brenda Knight, Ame Beanland, Martha Newton Furman and Suzanne Albertson in the design department who have rubbed this project on their in-house touchstone to ensure its beauty, and finally a bow and hand-to-the-heart thanks to my editor, Marianne Dresser, who has blessed this manuscript with her true peregrine spirit.

Most of all, heart-brimming thanks to my two-year-old son Jack, who has revealed to me the joy of seeing the world through the eyes of a sojourning child; and to my companion of many ancient highways, Jo Beaton, who keeps beguiling my pilgrim soul home.

PERMISSIONS

RECOMMENDED READING

Alexander's Path: A Travel Memoir, by Freya Stark. London: J. Murray, 1958.

Amazing Traveler: Isabella Bird, by Evelyn Kaye. Boulder, CO: Blue Penguin Publications, 1994.

American Places, by William Zinsser. New York: HarperCollins, 1992.

The Archetype of Pilgrimage: Outer Action with Inner Meaning, by Jean Dalby Clift and Wallace B. Clift. New York: Paulist Press, 1996.

An Artist's Book of Inspiration, by Astrid Fitzgerald. Hudson, NY: Lindisfarne Press, 1996.

The Art of Good Living: Simple Steps to Regaining Health and the Joy of Life, by Svevo Brooks. New York: Houghton Mifflin, 1986.

The Art of Writing: Teachings of the Chinese Masters, translated by Tony Barnstone and Chou Ping. Boston & London: Shambhala, 1996.

The Atlas of Holy Places and Sacred Sites, by Colin Wilson. London: Dorling Kindersley Ltd., 1996.

A Trail Through Leaves: The Journal as a Path to Place, by Hannah Hinchman. New York: W. W. Norton & Company, 1997.

A Book of Luminous Things: An International Anthology of Poetry, edited and with an introduction by Czeslaw Milosz. Orlando, FL: Harcourt Brace & Company, 1996.

Beyond the Grand Tour, by Hugh Tregaskis. London: Ascent Books, 1979.

The Call, by David Spangler. New York: Riverhead Books, 1997.

Callings: Finding and Following an Authentic Life, by Grey Levoy. New York: Harmony Books, 1997.

Classic Travel Stories, with an introduction by Fiona Pitt-Kethley. London: Leopard Press, 1996.

The Colossus of Maroussi, by Henry Miller. New York and London: Penguin Books, 1941.

The Courage to Create, by Rollo May. New York: W. W. Norton and Company, 1975.

Earth, Air, Fire, and Water, by Alexander Eliot. New York: Simon & Schuster, 1962.

Finding Flow: The Psychology of Engagement with Everyday Life, by Mihaly Csikszentmihaly. New York: Basic Books, 1997.

Four Quartets, by T. S. Eliot. New York: Harcourt Brace and Jovanovich, 1971.

Fried Eggs with Lace: A Family Poem, by Richard Beban. Venice, CA: Canned Spaghetti Press, 1996.

The Fruitful Darkness, by Joan Halifax. San Francisco: HarperSanFrancisco, 1993.

The Grand Tour, edited by Sheila Pickles. New York: Harmony House, 1990.

Gratefulness, the Heart of Prayer, by Brother David Steindl-Rast. Ramsey, NJ: Paulist Press, 1984.

The Great Travelers, edited by Milton Rugoff. New York: Simon & Schuster, 1960.

Grand Tours and Cook's Tours: A History of Leisure Travel: 1750–1915, by Lynne Withey. New York: William Morrow and Company, Inc., 1996.

A Haiku Journey: Basho's Narrow Road to a Far Province, translated by Dorothy Britten. Tokyo, New York & San Francisco: Kodansha International, 1980.

History of Travel, by Winfried Löschburg. Leipzig, Germany: Hippocrene Books, Inc., 1982.

The Hero's Journey: Joseph Campbell on his Life and Work, edited by Phil Cousineau. San Francisco: HarperSanFrancisco, 1990.

I Sailed with Rasmussen, by Peter Freuchen. New York: Viking Press, 1958.

Japanese Pilgrimage, by Oliver Statler. London: Picador Books, 1984.

The Journey of Light, by James Wright. New York: White Pine Press, 1972.

The Last Home of Mystery, by E. Alexander Powell. New York: The Sun Dial Press, 1939.

Last Words, by Antler. New York: Ballantine Books, 1986.

Letters to a Young Poet, by Rainer Maria Rilke. Translated by M. D. Herter Norton. New York: W. W. Norton & Company, 1962.

A Listening Heart: The Art of Contemplative Living, by Brother David Steindl-Rast. New York: Crossroads, 1992.

Loneliness and Time: The Story of British Travel Writing, by Mark Cocker. New York: Pantheon Books, 1992.

Longing for Darkness: Tara and the Black Madonna, by China Galland. New York: Penguin Books, 1990.

Maiden Voyages: Writings of Women Travelers, edited and with an introduction by Mary Morris, in collaboration with Larry O'Connor. New York: Vintage Books, 1993.

A Manual for Living, by Epictetus. An interpretation by Sharon Lebell. San Francisco: HarperSanFrancisco, 1994.

The Marvels of Rome, translated and edited by Francis Morgan Nichols. New York: Italica Press, 1986.

The Mind of the Traveler: From Gilgamesh to Global Tourism, by Eric J. Leed. New York: Basic Books, 1991.

Mount Analogue, by René Daumal. London: Penguin Books, 1959.

A Muriel Rukeyser Reader, edited by Jan Heller Levi with an introduction by Adrienne Rich. New York: W. W. Norton & Company, 1995.

My Life as an Explorer, by Sven Hedin. Translated by Alfhild Huebsch. New York: Kodansha International, 1996.

The Mystic Vision: Daily Encounters with the Divine, compiled by Andrew Harvey and Anne Baring. San Francisco: HarperSanFrancisco: 1995.

My Quest for Beauty, by Rollo May. San Francisco: Saybrook Publishing Company, 1985.

The Names of Things: A Passage in the Egyptian Desert, by Susan Brind Morrow. New York: Riverhead Books, 1997.

One Thousand Roads to Mecca, edited by Michael Wolfe. New York: Grove Press, 1997.

On Glory Roads: A Pilgrim's Book About Pilgrimage, by Eleanor Munro. London: Thames & Hudson, 1987.

On Pilgrimage, by Douglas C. Vest. Cambridge: Cowley Publications, 1998.

The Outermost House: A Year of Life on the Great Beach of Cape Cod, by Henry Beston. New York: Henry Holt & Co., 1988.

The Passionate Sightseer: From the Diaries 1947–1956, by Bernard Berenson. New York: Thames & Hudson, 1960.

Passion for Pilgrimage: Notes for the Journey Home, by Alan Jones. San Francisco: HarperSanFrancisco, 1989.

The Path to Rome, by Hilaire Belloc. Washington, DC: Gateway Editions, 1987.

Peace Pilgrim: Her Life and Work in Her Own Words, by Peace Pilgrim. Santa Monica, CA: Ocean Tree, 1994.

Pilgrimage in Ireland, by Peter Harrison. Syracuse, NY: University of Syracuse Press, 1992.

Pilgrimage: Past and Present in the World Religions, by Simon Coleman and John Elsner. Cambridge, MA: Harvard University Press, 1995.

Pilgrim of the Clouds: Poems and Essays from Ming China, by Yuan Hung-tao. Translated by Jonathan Chaves. New York and Tokyo: Inklings Press, 1978.

The Pilgrim's Guide to Santiago de Compostela, translated and with introduction, commentaries, and notes by William Melczer. New York: Italica Press, 1993.

Pilgrim's Road: A Journey to Santiago de Compostela, by Bettina Selby. London: Abacus Books, 1994.

The Pleasure of Ruins, by Rose Macauley, with photographs by Roloff Beny. New York: Holt, Rinehart & Winston, 1972.

Rasa: or Knowledge of the Self, by René Daumal. New York: New
    Directions, 1982.

The Road That Is Not a Road: And the Open City, Ritoque, Chile, by
    Ann M. Pendleton-Jullian. Chicago: Graham Foundation for
    Advanced Study in the Fine Arts, 1996.

The Road to Zion: Travellers to Palestine and the Land of Israel, by R. D.
    Kernohan. Edinburgh: The Handsel Press Ltd., 1995.

The Road Within: True Stories of Transformation, edited by Sean
    O'Reilly, James O'Reilly, and Tim O'Reilly. San Francisco:
    Travelers Tales, Inc., 1997.

The Sacred and the Profane: The Nature of Religion, by Mircea Eliade.
    Translated from the French by Willard R. Trask. New York:
    Harcourt, Brace & World, Inc., 1957.

Sacred Architecture, by A. T. Mann. Shaftesbury: Element Books Ltd.,
    1993.

Sacred Journeys, by Jennifer Westwood. New York: Henry Holt, 1997.

Sacred Mountains of the World, by Edwin Bernbaum. San Francisco:
    Sierra Club Books, 1990.

Sacred Places, Pilgrim Paths: An Anthology of Pilgrimage, by Martin
    Robinson. New York: HarperCollins, 1995.

Seamus Heaney: Selected Poems, 1966–1987. New York: Noonday
    Press, 1990.

The Songlines, by Bruce Chatwin. New York: Penguin, 1987.

Soul: An Archaeology: Readings from Socrates to Ray Charles, edited by
    Phil Cousineau. San Francisco: HarperSanFrancisco, 1994.

The Soul of the World: A Modern Book of Hours, edited by Phil Cousineau, with photographs by Eric Lawton. San Francisco: HarperSanFrancisco, 1992.

The Spiritual Quest, by Robert M. Torrance. Berkeley, CA: University of California Press, 1994.

Strange Pilgrims, by Gabriel García Márquez. Translated by Edith Grossman. New York: Alfred A. Knopf, 1993.

The Temple in the House, by Anthony Lawlor. New York: J. P. Tarcher, 1994.

Time and the Art of Living, by Robert Grudin. New York: Ticknor & Fields, 1988.

Time and the Soul, by Jacob Needleman. New York: Currency/ Doubleday, 1998.

The Traveler's Dictionary of Quotations: Who Said What, About Where?, edited by Peter Yapp. London: Rutledge & Kegan Paul, 1983.

Traveler's Joy: A Personal Guide to the Wonders and Pleasures of Gypsy and Nomad Living, by Juliette de Bairacli Levy. New Canaan, CT: Keats Publishing, Inc. 1979.

Walden, by Henry David Thoreau. Roslyn, NY: Walter J. Black, Inc., 1942.

Walking, by Henry David Thoreau. San Francisco: HarperSanFrancisco, 1995.

Walking A Sacred Path: Rediscovering the Labyrinth as a Spiritual Tool, by Lauren Artress. New York: Riverhead Books, 1995.

The Way of the Sacred, by Francis Huxley. New York: Dell Publishing, Inc., 1974.

Wherever You Go, There You Are: Mindfulness Meditation in Everyday Life, by Jon Kabat-Zinn. New York: Hyperion, 1994.

Women of the Beat Generation, by Brenda Knight. Berkeley, CA: Conari Press, 1996.

Yet Being Someone Other, by Laurens van der Post. New York: Penguin Books, 1984.

LIST OF ILLUSTRATIONS

Frontispiece: "Four Monks," Angkor Wat, Cambodia. Photograph by Phil Cousineau, 1996.

xvi: "Camel driver," Giza, Egypt. Photograph by Phil Cousineau, 1974.

xvii: "Be Safe and Well: Peace, Love, Courage," original Arabic script written by Ahmet on a cigarette card given to the author in London, 1974.

xix: "Sphinx and Pyramids," Giza, Egypt. Photograph by Phil Cousineau, 1974.

1: "The Angkor Wat Causeway," Angkor Wat, Cambodia. Photograph by Phil Cousineau, 1996.

3. "Buddhist nun at the Bayon," Angkor Thom, Cambodia. Photograph by Phil Cousineau, 1996.

7. "The Terrace of the Leper King," Angkor Wat, Cambodia. Photograph by Phil Cousineau, 1996.

10. The Mosque at Mecca. Bettman Archive.

12. Passport and stamps. Personal collection of the author.

14. "Wandering Bohemian" postcard. Personal collection of the author.

16. "The Spiritual Pilgrim." Adapted from a sixteenth-century German woodcut.

17. George Whitman, Paris, France. Photograph by Phil Cousineau, 1997.

19. Ruins of Glatsonbury Abbey, Glatsonbury, England. Photograph by Phil Cousineau, 1985.

31. "Tahquamenon Falls, Michigan." Photograph by Phil Cousineau, 1970.

33. "Wooden boats," Prague, Czech Republic. Photograph by Phil Cousineau, 1995.

35. "The Amphitheater," Ephesus, Turkey. Photograph by Phil Cousineau, 1990.

38. "The Practice of Mindfulness," Sukhothai, Thailand. Photograph by Phil Cousineau, 1983.

42. "The Reflection," Athens, Greece. Photograph by Phil Cousineau, 1992.

45. Right: "Silhouetted Crosses," Siauliai, Lithuania. Above: "The Offering," Siauliai, Lithuania. Photographs by Phil Cousineau, 1996.

49. "Poets." Photograph by Phil Cousineau, 1985.

50. "Contemplation," Chichen Itza, Yucatan, Mexico. Photograph by Phil Cousineau, 1994.

55. "The Tower of Samarra," Samarra, Iraq. Photograph by Dr. E. M. Bruins.

57. "The Philosopher." Photograph by Phil Cousineau, 1996.

59. "Les Voyageurs." Photograph by Phil Cousineau, 1995.

61. "The House of the Ancestors," Canyon de Chelly, Arizona. Photograph by Phil Cousineau, 1993.

64. "Buddha Foot Stones." From *Outlines of Chinese Symbolism and Art Motives*, Shanghai, 1932.

135. "Lost," San Francisco, California. Photograph by Jo Beaton, 1988.

139. "The Dove of Peace," Greenham Common RAF base, England. Photograph by Jo Beaton, 1985.

143. "The Last Song," Père-Lachaise cemetery, Paris, France. Photograph by Phil Cousineau, 1987.

147. "The Temple of the Sun," Tikal, Guatemala. Photograph by Phil Cousineau, 1993.

151. "The Tower," Grace Cathedral, San Francisco. Photograph by Phil Cousineau, 1996.

159. "The Temple of Apollo," Delphi, Greece. Photograph by Phil Cousineau, 1995.

164. "The Heartbeat of the World," Epidaurus, Greece. Photograph by Jo Beaton, 1992.

170. "Relics," Topkapi Museum, Istanbul, Turkey. Photograph by Phil Cousineau, 1990.

174. Detail from "Night Snow at Kambara," Utagawa Hiroshige (1797–1858). Original *ukiyo-e* print from the personal collection of Stanley H. Cousineau.

176. "The Pilgrim." Traditional print, artist unknown. Cited in *Japanese Pilgrimage,* by Oliver Statler.

179. "Silence," Le Thoronet Abbey, Provence, France. Photograph by Phil Cousineau, 1997.

199. "The Scaean Gates," Troy, Turkey. Photograph by Phil Cousineau, 1992.

229. "The Pilgrim's Hostel," Angkor Wat, Cambodia. Photograph by Phil Cousineau, 1996.

231. "The Path and the Pilgrim." Angkor Wat, Cambodia. Photograph by Phil Cousineau, 1996.

233. "Stone Swirls," Oxford, England. Photograph by Phil Cousineau, 1980.

ABOUT THE AUTHOR

PHIL COUSINEAU WAS BORN IN 1952 at the Fort Jackson army hospital in Columbia, South Carolina and grew up in Wayne, Michigan. While moonlighting in an automotive parts factory, he studied journalism at the University of Detroit. His peripatetic career has included sports writing, playing basketball in Europe, harvesting date trees on an Israeli kibbutz, painting forty-four Victorian houses in San Francisco, and leading adventure travel tours around the world.

Cousineau is an author, editor, photographer, tour leader, teacher, and documentary filmmaker. His lifelong fascination with art, literature, and the history of culture has taken him on journeys around the world. He lectures frequently on a wide range of topics including: mythology, movies, environmental design, community work, creativity, mentorship, and soul.

He is the author of several books including *Wordcatcher: An Odyssey into the World of Weird and Wonderful Words*; *Stoking the Creative Fires: 9 Ways to Rekindle Passion and Imagination*; *Once and Future Myths: The Power of Ancient Stories in Modern Times*; *The Hero's Journey: Joseph Campbell on His Life and Work*; *The Soul Aflame: A Modern Book of Hours*; and *The Way Things Are: Conversations with Huston Smith on the Spiritual Life*. He has also authored two books of poetry, *Night Train* and *The Blue Museum*, and has contributed to dozens of other books including John Densmore's *Riders on the Storm: My Life With Jim Morrison and the Doors*.

Cousineau's screenwriting credits in documentary films, which have won more than twenty-five international awards, include *Ecological Design: Inventing the Future*; *The Peyote Road*; *The Red Road to Sobriety*; *Your Humble Serpent: The Life of Reuben Snake*; *Wiping the Tears of Seven Generations*; *Eritrea: March to Freedom*; *The Presence of the Goddess*; *The Hero's Journey: The World of Joseph Campbell*; and the 1991

Academy Award-nominated *Forever Activists: Stories from the Abraham Lincoln Brigade.*

Cousineau currently hosts the PBS show *Global Spirit,* an "internal travel" television series. He lives in the North Beach neighborhood of San Francisco, California. Visit him online at www.philcousineau.net.

For more information on Phil Cousineau's art and literary tours and organized pilgrimages, please contact:

Sisyphus Travels
P. O. Box 330098
San Francisco, CA 94133

Conari Press, an imprint of Red Wheel/Weiser,
publishes books on topics ranging from spirituality,
personal growth, and relationships to women's issues, parenting,
and social issues. Our mission is to publish quality books
that will make a difference in people's lives—how we feel
about ourselves and how we relate to one another.
We value integrity, compassion, and receptivity,
both in the books we publish and in the way
we do business.

Our readers are our most important resource, and we value
your input, suggestions, and ideas about what you
would like to see published. Please feel free to contact us,
to request our latest book catalog, or to be added to our
mailing list.

Conari Press
an imprint of Red Wheel/Weiser, LLC
665 Third Street, Suite 400
San Francisco, CA 94107
www.redwheelweiser.com